ZEN MIND,
BEGINNER'S MIND

ZEN MIND, BEGINNER'S MIND

SHUNRYU SUZUKI

edited by Trudy Dixon
with a preface by Huston Smith
an introduction by Richard Baker
and an afterword by David Chadwick

SHAMBHALA
Boulder
2011

FRONTISPIECE: THE CHARACTERS FOR "BEGINNER'S MIND"
IN CALLIGRAPHY BY SHUNRYU SUZUKI.

Shambhala Publications, Inc.
4720 Walnut Street
Boulder, Colorado 80301
www.shambhala.com

14 13 12 11 10 9

Printed in the United States of America

♾ This edition is printed on acid-free paper that meets the
American National Standards Institute z39.48 Standard.
♻ This book is printed on 30% postconsumer recycled paper.
For more information please visit www.shambhala.com.
Distributed in the United States by Penguin Random House LLC
and in Canada by Random House of Canada Ltd

THE LIBRARY OF CONGRESS CATALOGUES THE PREVIOUS EDITION
OF THIS BOOK AS FOLLOWS:

Suzuki, Shunryu, 1904–1971
Zen mind, beginner's mind / Shunryu Suzuki; edited by Trudy Dixon, with a
preface by Huston Smith, an introduction by Richard Baker, and an afterword
by David Chadwick.—40th anniversary ed.
p. cm.
ISBN 978-1-59030-850-9 (hardcover: alk. paper)
ISBN 978-1-59030-890-5 (hardcover with slipcase: alk. paper)
ISBN 978-1-59030-849-3 (paperback: alk. paper)
1. Meditation—Zen Buddhism. 2. Zen Buddhism—Doctrines. I. Dixon,
Trudy. II. Title.
BQ9288.S994 2010
294.3'4435—dc22
2010023230

CONTENTS

PREFACE

Two Suzukis. A half-century ago, in a transplant that has been likened in its historical importance to the Latin translations of Aristotle in the thirteenth century and of Plato in the fifteenth, Daisetz Suzuki brought Zen to the West single-handed. Fifty years later, Shunryu Suzuki did something almost as important. He sounded exactly the follow-up note Americans interested in Zen need to hear.

Whereas Daisetz Suzuki's Zen was dramatic, Shunryu Suzuki's is ordinary. *Satori* was focal for Daisetz, and it was in large part the fascination of this extraordinary state that made his writings so compelling. In Shunryu Suzuki's book the words *satori* and *kensho,* its near-equivalent, never appear.

When, four months before his death, I had the opportunity to ask him why *satori* didn't figure in his book, his wife leaned toward me and whispered impishly, "It's because he hasn't had it"; whereupon the Roshi batted his fan at her in mock consternation and with finger to his lips hissed, "Shhhh! Don't tell him!" When our laughter had subsided, he said simply, "It's not that *satori* is unimportant, but it's not the part of Zen that needs to be stressed."

Suzuki-roshi was with us, in America, only twelve years—a single round in the East Asian way of counting years in dozens—but they were enough. Through the work of this

small, quiet man there is now a thriving Soto Zen organization on our continent. His life represented the Soto
Way so perfectly that the man and the Way were merged.
"His nonego attitude left us no eccentricities to embroi-
der upon. Though he made no waves and left no traces
as a personality in the worldly sense, the impress of his
footsteps in the invisible world of history lead straight
on."* His monuments are the first Soto Zen monastery in
the West, the Zen Mountain Center at Tassajara; its city
adjunct, the Zen Center in San Francisco; and, for the pub-
lic at large, this book.

Leaving nothing to chance, he prepared his students for
their most difficult moment, when his palpable presence
would vanish into the void:

> If when I die, the moment I'm dying, if I suffer
> that is all right, you know; that is suffering Bud-
> dha. No confusion in it. Maybe everyone will
> struggle because of the physical agony or spiri-
> tual agony, too. But that is all right, that is not
> a problem. We should be very grateful to have
> a limited body . . . like mine, or like yours. If
> you had a limitless life it would be a real prob-
> lem for you.

And he secured the transmission. In the Mountain Seat
ceremony, November 21, 1971, he installed Richard Baker
as his Dharma heir. His cancer had advanced to the point
where he could march in the processional only supported

*From a tribute by Mary Farkas in *Zen Notes*, the First Zen Institute of
America, January 1972.

by his son. Even so, with each step his staff banged the floor with the steel of the Zen will that informed his gentle exterior. Baker received the mantle with a poem:

> This piece of incense
> Which I have had for a long long time
> I offer with no-hand
> To my Master, to my friend, Suzuki Shunryu Daiosho
> The founder of these temples.
> There is no measure of what you have done.
>
> Walking with you in Buddha's gentle rain
> Our robes are soaked through,
> But on the lotus leaves
> Not a drop remains.

Two weeks later the Master was gone, and at his funeral on December 4 Baker-roshi spoke for the throng that had assembled to pay tribute:

> There is no easy way to be a teacher or a disciple, although it must be the greatest joy in this life. There is no easy way to come to a land without Buddhism and leave it having brought many disciples, priests, and laymen well along the path and having changed the lives of thousands of persons throughout this country; no easy way to have started and nurtured a monastery, a city community, and practice centers in California and many other places in the United States. But this "no-easy-way," this extraordinary accomplishment, rested easily with him, for he gave us from his own

true nature, our true nature. He left us as much as any man can leave, everything essential, the mind and heart of Buddha, the practice of Buddha, the teaching and life of Buddha. He is here in each one of us, if we want him.

HUSTON SMITH
Professor of Philosophy
Massachusetts Institute of Technology

INTRODUCTION

FOR A DISCIPLE of Suzuki-roshi, this book will be Suzuki-roshi's mind—not his ordinary mind or personal mind, but his Zen mind, the mind of his teacher Gyokujun So-on-daiosho, the mind of Dogen-zenji, the mind of the entire succession—broken or unbroken, historical and mythical—of teachers, patriarchs, monks, and laymen from Buddha's time until today, and it will be the mind of Buddha himself, the mind of Zen practice. But, for most readers, the book will be an example of how a Zen master talks and teaches. It will be a book of instruction about how to practice Zen, about Zen life, and about the attitudes and understanding that make Zen practice possible. For any reader, the book will be an encouragement to realize his own nature, his own Zen mind.

Zen mind is one of those enigmatic phrases used by Zen teachers to make you notice yourself, to go beyond the words and wonder what your own mind and being are. This is the purpose of all Zen teaching—to make you wonder and to answer that wondering with the deepest expression of your own nature. The calligraphy on the front of the binding reads *nyorai* in Japanese or *tathagata* in Sanskrit. This is a name for Buddha which means "he who has followed the path, who has returned from suchness, or is suchness, thus-ness, is-ness, emptiness, the fully completed one." It is the ground principle which makes the appearance of a Buddha possible. It is Zen mind. At the time Suzuki-roshi wrote this calligraphy—using for a brush the frayed end of one of the large swordlike leaves of the yucca plants that grow in the mountains around Zen Mountain Center—he said: "This means that Tathagata is the body of the whole earth."

The practice of Zen mind is beginner's mind. The innocence of the first inquiry—what am I?—is needed throughout Zen practice. The mind of the beginner is empty, free of the habits of the expert, ready to accept, to doubt, and open to all the possibilities. It is the kind of mind which can see things as they are, which step by step and in a flash can realize the original nature of everything. This practice of Zen mind is found throughout the book. Directly or by inference, every section of the book concerns the question of how to maintain beginner's mind through your meditation and in your life. This is an ancient way of teaching, using the simplest language and the situations of everyday life. This means the student should teach himself.

Beginner's mind was a favorite expression of Dogenzenji's. The calligraphy of the frontispiece, also by Suzuki-roshi, reads *shoshin,* or beginner's mind. The Zen way of calligraphy is to write in the most straightforward, simple way as if you were a beginner, not trying to make something skillful or beautiful, but simply writing with full attention as if you were discovering what you were writing for the first time; then your full nature will be in your writing. This is the way of practice moment after moment.

This book was conceived and initiated by Marian Derby, a close disciple of Suzuki-roshi and organizer of the Los Altos Zen group. Suzuki-roshi joined the zazen meditations of this group once or twice a week, and after each meditation period he would talk to them, encouraging their practice and helping them with their problems. Marian taped his talks and soon saw that as the group developed the talks acquired a continuity and development which would work well as a book and could be a much-needed record of Suzuki-roshi's remarkable spirit and teaching. From her transcriptions of talks made over a period of several years, she put together the first draft of the present book.

Then Trudy Dixon, another close disciple of Suzuki-roshi who had much experience editing Zen Center's publication, *Wind Bell,* edited and organized the manuscript for publication. It is no easy task to edit this kind of book, and explaining why will help the reader understand the book better. Suzuki-roshi takes the most difficult but persuasive way to talk about Buddhism—in terms of the ordinary circumstances of people's lives—to try to convey the whole of the teaching in statements as simple as "Have a cup of tea." The editor must be aware of the implications behind such statements in order not to edit out for the sake of clarity or grammar the real meaning of the lectures. Also, without knowing Suzuki-roshi well and having experience working with him, it is easy to edit out for the same reasons the background understanding that is his personality or energy or will. And it is also easy to edit out the deeper mind of the reader which needs the repetition, the seemingly obscure logic, and the poetry in order to know itself. Passages which seem obscure or obvious are often illuminating when they are read very carefully, wondering why this man would say such a thing.

The editing is further complicated by the fact that English is thoroughly dualistic in its basic assumptions and has not had the opportunity over centuries to develop a way of expressing nondualistic Buddhist ideas, as has Japanese. Suzuki-roshi uses these different cultural vocabularies freely, expressing himself in both Japanese and Western ways of thinking. In his lectures, they merge poetically and philosophically. But in transcriptions, the pauses, rhythm, and emphasis that give his words their deeper meaning and hold his thoughts together are apt to be lost. So Trudy worked many months by herself and with Suzuki-roshi to retain his original words and flavor, and yet produce a manuscript that is in understandable English.

Trudy divided the book according to emphasis into three sections—Right Practice, Right Attitude, and Right Understanding—roughly corresponding to body, feeling, and mind. She also chose the titles for the talks and the epigraphs that follow the titles, these being taken usually from the body of the lectures. The choices are of course somewhat arbitrary, but she did this to set up a kind of tension between the specific sections, titles, and epigraphs, and the talks themselves. The relationship between the talks and these added elements will help the reader probe the lectures. The only talk not given originally to the Los Altos group is the Epilogue, which is a condensation of two talks given when Zen Center moved into its new San Francisco headquarters.

Shortly after finishing work on this book, Trudy died of cancer at the age of thirty. She is survived by her two children, Annie and Will, and her husband, Mike, a painter. He contributed the drawing of the fly on page 55. A Zen student for many years, when asked to do something for this book, he said: "I can't do a Zen drawing. I can't do a drawing for anything other than the drawing. I certainly can't see doing drawings of *zafu* [meditation pillows] or lotuses or ersatz something. I can see this idea, though." A realistic fly often occurs in Mike's paintings. Suzuki-roshi is very fond of the frog, which sits so still it might be asleep, but is alert enough to notice every insect that comes by. Maybe the fly is waiting for the frog.

Trudy and I worked together throughout the development of *Zen Mind, Beginner's Mind,* and she asked me to complete the editing and see the book through to publication. After considering several publishers, I found that John Weatherhill, Inc., through Meredith Weatherby and Audie Bock, were able to polish, design, and publish this book in exactly the way it should be published. The manuscript was read before publication by Professor Kogen Mizuno, head of the Buddhist Studies Department, Komazawa University, and an outstanding scholar of Indian Buddhism. He generously helped with the transliteration of the Sanskrit and Japanese Buddhist terms.

Except for now and again in lectures, Suzuki-roshi seldom talks about his past, but this much I have pieced together. He was the disciple of Gyokujun So on-roshi. He had other teachers; the most influential for him was Kishizawa Ian-roshi, a leading authority and lecturer on Dogen. Kishizawa-roshi emphasized a deep and careful understanding of Dogen, the koans—particularly the *Blue Cliff Records*—and the sutras. Suzuki Roshi was twelve when he began his apprenticeship under his father's disciple, Gyokujun. After years living with his teacher, he continued his practice and study at a Buddhist university, Komazawa, and at the main Soto training monasteries, Eiheiji and Sojiji. He also studied with a Rinzai teacher for awhile.

Gyokujun-roshi died when Suzuki was thirty. As a result, he had the responsibility, at a rather young age, of both his father's temple (who had died shortly before Gyokujun) and his teacher's temple. The latter, Rinsoin, was a small monastery and head temple for about two hundred other temples. One of his main tasks was the rebuilding of Rinsoin in the exacting tradition his teacher and he wanted.

Exceptional for Japan during the nineteen thirties and forties, he led discussion groups at Rinsoin that questioned the militaristic assumptions and actions of the times. Before the war, and from the time he was young, he had been interested in coming to America; however, at the insistence of his teacher, he had given up the idea. But in 1956 and twice again in '58, a friend, who was one of the leaders of the Soto School, persisted in asking him to go to San Francisco to lead the Japanese Soto congregation there. On the third request, Suzuki-roshi accepted.

In 1959, when he was fifty-five, he came to America. After postponing his return several times, he decided to stay in America. He stayed because he found that Americans have a beginner's mind, that they have few preconceptions about Zen, are quite open to it, and confidently believe that it can help their lives. He found they question Zen in a way that gives Zen life. Shortly after his arrival several people stopped by and asked if they could study Zen with him. He said he did zazen early every morning and they could join him if they liked. Since then a rather large Zen group has grown up around him—now in six locations in California. At present he spends most of his time at Zen Center, 300 Page Street, San Francisco, where about sixty students live and many more do zazen regularly, and at Zen Mountain Center at Tassajara Springs above Carmel Valley. This latter is the first Zen monastery in America, and there another sixty or so students live and practice for three-month or longer periods.

Trudy felt that understanding how Zen students feel about their teacher might, more than anything else, help the reader to understand these talks. What the teacher really offers the student is literally living proof that all this talk and the seemingly impossible goals can be realized in this lifetime. The deeper you go in your practice, the deeper you find your teacher's mind is, until you finally see that your mind and his mind are Buddha's mind. And you find that zazen meditation is the most perfect expression of your actual nature. The following tribute from Trudy to her teacher describes very well the relationship between Zen teacher and Zen student:

"A roshi is a person who has actualized that perfect freedom which is the potentiality for all human beings. He exists freely in the fullness of his whole being. The flow of his consciousness is not the fixed repetitive patterns of our usual self-centered consciousness, but rather arises spontaneously and naturally from the actual circumstances of the present. The results of this in terms of the quality of his life are extraordinary—buoyancy, vigor, straightforwardness, simplicity, humility, serenity, joyousness, uncanny perspicacity, and unfathomable compassion. His whole being testifies to what it means to live in the reality of the present. Without anything said or done, just the impact of meeting a personality so developed can be enough to change another's whole way of life. But in the end it is not the extraordinariness of the teacher which perplexes, intrigues, and deepens the student, it is the teacher's utter ordinariness. Because he is just himself, he is a mirror for his students. When we are with him we feel our own strengths and shortcomings without any sense of praise or criticism from him. In his presence we see our original face, and the extraordinariness we see is only our own true nature. When we learn to let our own nature free, the boundaries between master and student disappear in a deep flow of being and joy in the unfolding of Buddha mind."

RICHARD BAKER
Kyoto, 1970

ZEN MIND,
BEGINNER'S MIND

It is wisdom which is seeking for wisdom.

PROLOGUE

BEGINNER'S MIND *"In the beginner's mind there are many possibilities, but in the expert's there are few."*

People say that practicing Zen is difficult, but there is a misunderstanding as to why. It is not difficult because it is hard to sit in the cross-legged position, or to attain enlightenment. It is difficult because it is hard to keep our mind pure and our practice pure in its fundamental sense. The Zen school developed in many ways after it was established in China, but at the same time, it became more and more impure. But I do not want to talk about Chinese Zen or the history of Zen. I am interested in helping you keep your practice from becoming impure.

In Japan we have the phrase *shoshin,* which means "beginner's mind." The goal of practice is always to keep our beginner's mind. Suppose you recite the Prajna Paramita Sutra only once. It might be a very good recitation. But what would happen to you if you recited it twice, three times, four times, or more? You might easily lose your original attitude towards it. The same thing will happen in your other Zen practices. For a while you will keep your beginner's mind, but if you continue to practice one, two, three years or more, although you may improve some, you are liable to lose the limitless meaning of original mind.

For Zen students the most important thing is not to be dualistic. Our "original mind" includes everything within itself. It is always rich and sufficient within itself. You should not lose your self-sufficient state of mind. This does not mean a closed mind, but actually an empty mind and a ready mind. If your mind is empty, it is always ready for anything; it is open to everything. In the beginner's mind there are many possibilities; in the expert's mind there are few.

If you discriminate too much, you limit yourself. If you are too demanding or too greedy, your mind is not rich and self-sufficient. If we lose our original self-sufficient mind, we will lose all precepts. When your mind becomes demanding, when you long for something, you will end up violating your own precepts: not to tell lies, not to steal, not to kill, not to be immoral, and so forth. If you keep your original mind, the precepts will keep themselves.

In the beginner's mind there is no thought, "I have attained something." All self-centered thoughts limit our vast mind. When we have no thought of achievement, no thought of self, we are true beginners. Then we can really learn something. The beginner's mind is the mind of compassion. When our mind is compassionate, it is boundless. Dogen-zenji, the founder of our school, always emphasized how important it is to resume our boundless original mind. Then we are always true to ourselves, in sympathy with all beings, and can actually practice.

So the most difficult thing is always to keep your beginner's mind. There is no need to have a deep understanding of Zen. Even though you read much Zen literature, you must read each sentence with a fresh mind. You should not say, "I know what Zen is," or "I have attained enlightenment." This is also the real secret of the arts: always be a beginner. Be very very careful about this point. If you start to practice zazen, you will begin to appreciate your beginner's mind. It is the secret of Zen practice.

PART ONE

Right Practice

Zazen practice is the direct expression of our true nature. Strictly speaking, for a human being, there is no other practice than this practice; there is no other way of life than this way of life.

P OSTURE   *"These forms are not the means of obtaining the right state of mind. To take this posture is itself to have the right state of mind. There is no need to obtain some special state of mind."*

Now I would like to talk about our zazen posture. When you sit in the full lotus position, your left foot is on your right thigh, and your right foot is on your left thigh. When we cross our legs like this, even though we have a right leg and a left leg, they have become one. The position express-es the oneness of duality: not two, and not one. This is the most important teaching: not two, and not one. Our body and mind are not two and not one. If you think your body and mind are two, that is wrong; if you think that they are one, that is also wrong. Our body and mind are both two and one. We usually think that if something is not one, it is more than one; if it is not singular, it is plural. But in actual experience, our life is not only plural, but also singular. Each one of us is both dependent and independent.

After some years we will die. If we just think that it is the end of our life, this will be the wrong understanding. But, on the other hand, if we think that we do not die, this is also wrong. We die, and we do not die. This is the right under-standing. Some people may say that our mind or soul ex-ists forever, and it is only our physical body which dies. But this is not exactly right, because both mind and body have their end. But at the same time it is also true that they exist eternally. And even though we say mind and body, they are actually two sides of one coin. This is the right understanding. So when we take this posture it symbolizes this truth. When I have the left foot on the right side of my body, and the right foot on the left side of my body, I do not know which is which. So either may be the left or the right side.

The most important thing in taking the zazen posture is to keep your spine straight. Your ears and your shoulders should be on one line. Relax your shoulders, and push up towards the ceiling with the back of your head. And you should pull your chin in. When your chin is tilted up, you have no strength in your posture; you are probably dreaming. Also to gain strength in your posture, press your diaphragm down towards your *hara,* or lower abdomen. This will help you maintain your physical and mental balance. When you try to keep this posture, at first you may find some difficulty breathing naturally, but when you get accustomed to it you will be able to breathe naturally and deeply.

Your hands should form the "cosmic mudra." If you put your left hand on top of your right, middle joints of your middle fingers together, and touch your thumbs lightly together (as if you held a piece of paper between them), your hands will make a beautiful oval. You should keep this universal mudra with great care, as if you were holding something very precious in your hand. Your hands should be held against your body, with your thumbs at about the height of your navel. Hold your arms freely and easily, and slightly away from your body, as if you held an egg under each arm without breaking it.

You should not be tilted sideways, backwards, or forwards. You should be sitting straight up as if you were supporting the sky with your head. This is not just form or breathing. It expresses the key point of Buddhism. It is a

perfect expression of your Buddha nature. If you want true
understanding of Buddhism, you should practice this way.
These forms are not a means of obtaining the right state of
mind. To take this posture itself is the purpose of our practice. When you have this posture, you have the right state
of mind, so there is no need to try to attain some special
state. When you try to attain something, your mind starts
to wander about somewhere else. When you do not try to
attain anything, you have your own body and mind right
here. A Zen master would say, "Kill the Buddha!" Kill the
Buddha if the Buddha exists somewhere else. Kill the Buddha, because you should resume your own Buddha nature.

Doing something is expressing our own nature. We do
not exist for the sake of something else. We exist for the
sake of ourselves. This is the fundamental teaching expressed in the forms we observe. Just as for sitting, when
we stand in the zendo we have some rules. But the purpose
of these rules is not to make everyone the same, but to allow each to express his own self most freely. For instance,
each one of us has his own way of standing, so our standing posture is based on the proportions of our own bodies.
When you stand, your heels should be as far apart as the
width of your own fist, your big toes in line with the cen-
ters of your breasts. As in zazen, put some strength in your
abdomen. Here also your hands should express your self.
Hold your left hand against your chest with fingers encircl-
ing your thumb, and put your right hand over it. Holding
your thumb pointing downward, and your forearms paral-
lel to the floor, you feel as if you have some round pillar in
your grasp—a big round temple pillar—so you cannot be
slumped or tilted to the side.

The most important point is to own your own physical

body. If you slump, you will lose your self. Your mind will be wandering about somewhere else; you will not be in your body. This is not the way. We must exist right here, right now! This is the key point. You must have your own body and mind. Everything should exist in the right place, in the right way. Then there is no problem. If the microphone I use when I speak exists somewhere else, it will not serve its purpose. When we have our body and mind in order, everything else will exist in the right place, in the right way.

But usually, without being aware of it, we try to change something other than ourselves, we try to order things outside us. But it is impossible to organize things if you yourself are not in order. When you do things in the right way, at the right time, everything else will be organized. You are the "boss." When the boss is sleeping, everyone is sleeping. When the boss does something right, everyone will do everything right, and at the right time. That is the secret of Buddhism.

So try always to keep the right posture, not only when you practice zazen, but in all your activities. Take the right posture when you are driving your car, and when you are reading. If you read in a slumped position, you cannot stay awake long. Try. You will discover how important it is to keep the right posture. This is the true teaching. The teaching which is written on paper is not the true teaching. Written teaching is a kind of food for your brain. Of course it is necessary to take some food for your brain, but it is more important to be yourself by practicing the right way of life.

That is why Buddha could not accept the religions existing at his time. He studied many religions, but he was not satisfied with their practices. He could not find the answer in asceticism or in philosophies. He was not interested in some metaphysical existence, but in his own body and mind, here and now. And when he found himself, he found that everything that exists has Buddha nature. That was his enlightenment. Enlightenment is not some good feeling or some particular state of mind. The state of mind that exists when you sit in the right posture is, itself, enlightenment. If you cannot be satisfied with the state of mind you have in zazen, it means your mind is still wandering about. Our body and mind should not be wobbling or wandering about. In this posture there is no need to talk about the right state of mind. You already have it. This is the conclusion of Buddhism.

BREATHING   *"What we call 'I' is just a swinging door which moves when we inhale and when we exhale."*

When we practice zazen our mind always follows our breathing. When we inhale, the air comes into the inner world. When we exhale, the air goes out to the outer world. The inner world is limitless, and the outer world is also limitless. We say "inner world" or "outer world," but actually there is just one whole world. In this limitless world, our throat is like a swinging door. The air comes in and goes out like someone passing through a swinging door. If you think, "I breathe," the "I" is extra. There is no you to say "I." What we call "I" is just a swinging door which moves when we inhale and when we exhale. It just moves; that is all. When your mind is pure and calm enough to follow this movement, there is nothing: no "I," no world, no mind nor body; just a swinging door.

So when we practice zazen, all that exists is the movement of the breathing, but we are aware of this movement. You should not be absent-minded. But to be aware of the movement does not mean to be aware of your small self, but rather of your universal nature, or Buddha nature. This kind of awareness is very important, because we are usually so one-sided. Our usual understanding of life is dualistic: you and I, this and that, good and bad. But actually these discriminations are themselves the awareness of the universal existence. "You" means to be aware of the universe in the form of you, and "I" means to be aware of it in the form of I. You and I are just swinging doors. This kind of understanding is necessary. This should not even be called understanding; it is actually the true experience of life through Zen practice.

So when you practice zazen, there is no idea of time or space. You may say, "We started sitting at a quarter to six in this room." Thus you have some idea of time (a quarter to six), and some idea of space (in this room). Actually what you are doing, however, is just sitting and being aware of the universal activity. That is all. This moment the swinging door is opening in one direction, and the next moment the swinging door will be opening in the opposite direction. Moment after moment each one of us repeats this activity. Here there is no idea of time or space. Time and space are one. You may say, "I must do something this afternoon," but actually there is no "this afternoon." We do things one after the other. That is all. There is no such time as "this afternoon" or "one o'clock" or "two o'clock." At one o'clock you will eat your lunch. To eat lunch is itself one o'clock.

You will be somewhere, but that place cannot be separated from one o'clock. For someone who actually appreciates our life, they are the same. But when we become tired of our life we may say, "I shouldn't have come to this place. It may have been much better to have gone to some other place for lunch. This place is not so good." In your mind you create an idea of place separate from an actual time.

Or you may say, "This is bad, so I should not do this." Actually, when you say, "I should not do this," you are doing not-doing in that moment. So there is no choice for you. When you separate the idea of time and space, you feel as if you have some choice, but actually, you have to do something, or you have to do not-doing. Not-to-do something is doing something. Good and bad are only in your mind. So we should not say, "This is good," or "This is bad." Instead of saying bad, you should say, "not-to-do"! If you think, "This is bad," it will create some confusion for you. So in the realm of pure religion there is no confusion of time and space, or good or bad. All that we should do is just do something as it comes. *Do* something! Whatever it is, we should do it, even if it is not-doing something. We should live in this moment. So when we sit we concentrate on our breathing, and we become a swinging door, and we do something we should do, something we must do. This is Zen practice. In this practice there is no confusion. If you establish this kind of life you have no confusion whatsoever.

Tozan, a famous Zen master, said, "The blue mountain is the father of the white cloud. The white cloud is the son of the blue mountain. All day long they depend on each other, without being dependent on each other. The white cloud is always the white cloud. The blue mountain is always the blue mountain." This is a pure, clear interpretation of life.

There may be many things like the white cloud and blue mountain: man and woman, teacher and disciple. They depend on each other. But the white cloud should not be bothered by the blue mountain. The blue mountain should not be bothered by the white cloud. They are quite independent, but yet dependent. This is how we live, and how we practice zazen.

When we become truly ourselves, we just become a swinging door, and we are purely independent of, and at the same time, dependent upon everything. Without air, we cannot breathe. Each one of us is in the midst of myriads of worlds. We are in the center of the world always, moment after moment. So we are completely dependent and independent. If you have this kind of experience, this kind of existence, you have absolute independence; you will not be bothered by anything. So when you practice zazen, your mind should be concentrated on your breathing. This kind of activity is the fundamental activity of the universal being. Without this experience, this practice, it is impossible to attain absolute freedom.

CONTROL   *"To give your sheep or cow a large, spacious meadow is the way to control him."*

To live in the realm of Buddha nature means to die as a small being, moment after moment. When we lose our balance we die, but at the same time we also develop ourselves, we grow. Whatever we see is changing, losing its balance. The reason everything looks beautiful is because it is out of balance, but its background is always in perfect harmony. This is how everything exists in the realm of Buddha nature, losing its balance against a background of perfect balance. So if you see things without realizing the background of Buddha nature, everything appears to be in the form of suffering. But if you understand the background of existence, you realize that suffering itself is how we live, and how we extend our life. So in Zen sometimes we emphasize the imbalance or disorder of life.

Nowadays traditional Japanese painting has become pretty formal and lifeless. That is why modern art has developed. Ancient painters used to practice putting dots on paper in artistic disorder. This is rather difficult. Even though you try to do it, usually what you do is arranged in some order. You think you can control it, but you cannot; it is almost impossible to arrange your dots out of order. It is the same with taking care of your everyday life. Even though you try to put people under some control, it is impossible. You cannot do it. The best way to control people is to encourage them to be mischievous. Then they will be in control in its wider sense. To give your sheep or cow a large, spacious meadow is the way to control him. So it is with people: first let them do what they want, and watch them. This is the best policy. To ignore them is not good; that is the worst policy. The second worst is trying to control them. The best one is to watch them, just to watch them, without trying to control them.

The same way works for you yourself as well. If you want to obtain perfect calmness in your zazen, you should not be bothered by the various images you find in your mind. Let them come, and let them go. Then they will be under control. But this policy is not so easy. It sounds easy, but it requires some special effort. How to make this kind of effort is the secret of practice. Suppose you are sitting under some extraordinary circumstances. If you try to calm your mind you will be unable to sit, and if you try not to be disturbed, your effort will not be the right effort. The only effort that will help you is to count your breathing, or to concentrate on your inhaling and exhaling. We say concentration, but to concentrate your mind on something is not the true purpose of Zen. The true purpose is to see things as they are, to observe things as they are, and to let everything go as it goes. This is to put everything under control in its widest sense. Zen practice is to open up our small mind. So concentrating is just an aid to help you realize "big mind," or the mind that is everything. If you want to discover the true meaning of Zen in your everyday life, you have to understand the meaning of keeping your mind on your breathing and your body in the right posture in zazen. You should follow the rules of practice and your study should become more subtle and careful. Only in this way can you experience the vital freedom of Zen.

Dogen-zenji said, "Time goes from present to past." This is absurd, but in our practice sometimes it is true. Instead of time progressing from past to present, it goes backwards from present to past. Yoshitsune was a famous warrior who lived in medieval Japan. Because of the situation of the country at that time, he was sent to the northern provinces, where he was killed. Before he left he bade farewell to his wife, and soon after she wrote in a poem, "Just as you unreel the thread from a spool, I want the past to become present." When she said this, actually she made past time present. In her mind the past became alive and *was* the present. So as Dogen said, "Time goes from present to past." This is not true in our logical mind, but it is in the actual experience of making past time present. There we have poetry, and there we have human life.

When we experience this kind of truth it means we have found the true meaning of time. Time constantly goes from past to present and from present to future. This is true, but it is also true that time goes from future to present and from present to past. A Zen master once said, "To go eastward one mile is to go westward one mile." This is vital freedom. We should acquire this kind of perfect freedom.

But perfect freedom is not found without some rules. People, especially young people, think that freedom is to do just what they want, that in Zen there is no need for rules. But it is absolutely necessary for us to have some rules. But this does not mean always to be under control. As long as you have rules, you have a chance for freedom. To try to obtain freedom without being aware of the rules means nothing. It is to acquire this perfect freedom that we practice zazen.

M IND WAVES *"Because we enjoy all aspects of life as an unfolding of big mind, we do not care for any excessive joy. So we have imperturbable composure."*

When you are practicing zazen, do not try to stop your thinking. Let it stop by itself. If something comes into your mind, let it come in, and let it go out. It will not stay long. When you try to stop your thinking, it means you are bothered by it. Do not be bothered by anything. It appears as if something comes from outside your mind, but actually it is only the waves of your mind, and if you are not bothered by the waves, gradually they will become calmer and calmer. In five or at most ten minutes, your mind will be completely serene and calm. At that time your breathing will become quite slow, while your pulse will become a little faster.

It will take quite a long time before you find your calm, serene mind in your practice. Many sensations come, many thoughts or images arise, but they are just waves of your own mind. Nothing comes from outside your mind. Usually we think of our mind as receiving impressions and experiences from outside, but that is not a true understanding of our mind. The true understanding is that the mind includes everything; when you think something comes from outside it means only that something appears in your mind. Nothing outside yourself can cause any trouble. You yourself make the waves in your mind. If you leave your mind as it is, it will become calm. This mind is called big mind.

If your mind is related to something outside itself, that mind is a small mind, a limited mind. If your mind is not related to anything else, then there is no dualistic understanding in the activity of your mind. You understand activity as just waves of your mind. Big mind experiences everything within itself. Do you understand the difference between the two minds: the mind which includes everything, and the mind which is related to something? Actually they are the same thing, but the understanding is different, and your attitude towards your life will be different according to which understanding you have.

That everything is included within your mind is the essence of mind. To experience this is to have religious feeling. Even though waves arise, the essence of your mind is pure; it is just like clear water with a few waves. Actually water always has waves. Waves are the practice of the water. To speak of waves apart from water or water apart from waves is a delusion. Water and waves are one. Big mind and small mind are one. When you understand your mind in this way, you have some security in your feeling. As your mind does not expect anything from outside, it is always filled. A mind with waves in it is not a disturbed mind, but actually an amplified one. Whatever you experience is an expression of big mind.

The activity of big mind is to amplify itself through various experiences. In one sense our experiences coming one by one are always fresh and new, but in another sense they are nothing but a continuous or repeated unfolding of the one big mind. For instance, if you have something good for breakfast, you will say, "This is good." "Good" is supplied as something experienced some time long ago, even though you may not remember when. With big mind we accept each of our experiences as if recognizing the face we see in a mirror as our own. For us there is no fear of losing this mind. There is nowhere to come or to go; there is no fear of death, no suffering from old age or sickness. Because we enjoy all aspects of life as an unfolding of big mind, we do not care for any excessive joy. So we have imperturbable composure, and it is with this imperturbable composure of big mind that we practice zazen.

MIND WEEDS

"You should rather be grateful for the weeds you have in your mind, because eventually they will enrich your practice."

When the alarm rings early in the morning, and you get up, I think you do not feel so good. It is not easy to go and sit, and even after you arrive at the zendo and begin zazen you have to encourage yourself to sit well. These are just waves of your mind. In pure zazen there should not be any waves in your mind. While you are sitting these waves will become smaller and smaller, and your effort will change into some subtle feeling.

We say, "Pulling out the weeds we give nourishment to the plant." We pull the weeds and bury them near the plant to give it nourishment. So even though you have some difficulty in your practice, even though you have some waves while you are sitting, those waves themselves will help you. So you should not be bothered by your mind. You should rather be grateful for the weeds, because eventually they will enrich your practice. If you have some experience of how the weeds in your mind change into mental nourishment, your practice will make remarkable progress. You will feel the progress. You will feel how they change into self-nourishment. Of course it is not so difficult to give some philosophical or psychological interpretation of our practice, but that is not enough. We must have the actual experience of how our weeds change into nourishment.

Strictly speaking, any effort we make is not good for our practice because it creates waves in our mind. It is impossible, however, to attain absolute calmness of our mind without any effort. We must make some effort, but we must forget ourselves in the effort we make. In this realm there is no subjectivity or objectivity. Our mind is just calm, without even any awareness. In this unawareness, every effort and every idea and thought will vanish. So it is necessary for us to encourage ourselves and to make an effort up to the last moment, when all effort disappears. You should keep your mind on your breathing until you are not aware of your breathing.

We should try to continue our effort forever, but we should not expect to reach some stage when we will forget all about it. We should just try to keep our mind on our breathing. That is our actual practice. That effort will be refined more and more while you are sitting. At first the effort you make is quite rough and impure, but by the power of practice the effort will become purer and purer. When your effort becomes pure, your body and mind become pure. This is the way we practice Zen. Once you understand our innate power to purify ourselves and our surroundings, you can act properly, and you will learn from those around you, and you will become friendly with others. This is the merit of Zen practice. But the way of practice is just to be concentrated on your breathing with the right posture and with great, pure effort. This is how we practice Zen.

THE MARROW OF ZEN   *"In the zazen posture, your mind and body have great power to accept things as they are, whether agreeable or disagreeable."*

In our scriptures (Samyuktagama Sutra, volume 33), it is said that there are four kinds of horses: excellent ones, good ones, poor ones, and bad ones. The best horse will run slow and fast, right and left, at the driver's will, before it sees the shadow of the whip; the second best will run as well as the first one does, just before the whip reaches its skin; the third one will run when it feels pain on its body; the fourth will run after the pain penetrates to the marrow of its bones. You can imagine how difficult it is for the fourth one to learn how to run!

When we hear this story, almost all of us want to be the best horse. If it is impossible to be the best one, we want to be the second best. This is, I think, the usual understanding of this story, and of Zen. You may think that when you sit in zazen you will find out whether you are one of the best horses or one of the worst ones. Here, however, there is a misunderstanding of Zen. If you think the aim of Zen practice is to train you to become one of the best horses, you will have a big problem. This is not the right understanding. If you practice Zen in the right way it does not matter whether you are the best horse or the worst one. When you consider the mercy of Buddha, how do you think Buddha will feel about the four kinds of horses? He will have more sympathy for the worst one than for the best one.

When you are determined to practice zazen with the great mind of Buddha, you will find the worst horse is the most valuable one. In your very imperfections you will find the basis for your firm, way-seeking mind. Those who can sit perfectly physically usually take more time to obtain the true way of Zen, the actual feeling of Zen, the marrow of Zen. But those who find great difficulties in practicing Zen will find more meaning in it. So I think that sometimes the best horse may be the worst horse, and the worst horse can be the best one.

If you study calligraphy you will find that those who are not so clever usually become the best calligraphers. Those who are very clever with their hands often encounter great difficulty after they have reached a certain stage. This is also true in art and in Zen. It is true in life. So when we talk about Zen we cannot say, "He is good," or "He is bad," in the ordinary sense of the words. The posture taken in zazen is not the same for each of us. For some it may be impossible to take the cross-legged posture. But even though you cannot take the right posture, when you arouse your real, way-seeking mind, you can practice Zen in its true sense. Actually it is easier for those who have difficulties in sitting to arouse the true way-seeking mind than for those who can sit easily.

When we reflect on what we are doing in our everyday life, we are always ashamed of ourselves. One of my students wrote to me saying, "You sent me a calendar, and I am trying to follow the good mottoes which appear on each page. But the year has hardly begun, and already I have failed!" Dogen-zenji said, *"Shoshaku jushaku."* *Shaku* generally means "mistake" or "wrong." *Shoshaku jushaku* means "to succeed wrong with wrong," or one continuous mistake. According to Dogen, one continuous mistake can also be Zen. A Zen master's life could be said to be so many years of *shoshaku jushaku*. This means so many years of one single-minded effort.

We say, "A good father is not a good father." Do you understand? One who thinks he is a good father is not a good father; one who thinks he is a good husband is not a good husband. One who thinks he is one of the worst husbands may be a good one if he is always trying to be a good husband with a single-hearted effort. If you find it impossible to sit because of some pain or some physical difficulty, then you should sit anyway, using a thick cushion or a chair. Even though you are the worst horse you will get to the marrow of Zen.

Suppose your children are suffering from a hopeless disease. You do not know what to do; you cannot lie in bed. Normally the most comfortable place for you would be a warm comfortable bed, but now because of your mental agony you cannot rest. You may walk up and down, in and out, but this does not help. Actually the best way to relieve your mental suffering is to sit in zazen, even in such a confused state of mind and bad posture. If you have no experience of sitting in this kind of difficult situation you are not a Zen student. No other activity will appease your suffering. In other restless positions you have no power to accept your difficulties, but in the zazen posture which you have acquired by long, hard practice, your mind and body have great power to accept things as they are, whether they are agreeable or disagreeable.

When you feel disagreeable it is better for you to sit. There is no other way to accept your problem and work on it. Whether you are the best horse or the worst, or whether your posture is good or bad is out of the question. Everyone can practice zazen, and in this way work on his problems and accept them.

When you are sitting in the middle of your own problem, which is more real to you: your problem or you yourself? The awareness that you are here, right now, is the ultimate fact. This is the point you will realize by zazen practice. In continuous practice, under a succession of agreeable and disagreeable situations, you will realize the marrow of Zen and acquire its true strength.

N O DUALISM   *"To stop your mind does not mean to stop the activities of mind. It means your mind pervades your whole body. With your full mind you form the mudra in your hands."*

We say our practice should be without gaining ideas, without any expectations, even of enlightenment. This does not mean, however, just to sit without any purpose. This practice free from gaining ideas is based on the Prajna Paramita Sutra. However, if you are not careful the sutra itself will give you a gaining idea. It says, "Form is emptiness and emptiness is form." But if you attach to that statement, you are liable to be involved in dualistic ideas: here is you, form, and here is emptiness, which you are trying to realize through your form. So "form is emptiness, and emptiness is form" is still dualistic. But fortunately, our teaching goes on to say, "Form is form and emptiness is emptiness." Here there is no dualism.

When you find it difficult to stop your mind while you are sitting and when you are still trying to stop your mind, this is the stage of "form is emptiness and emptiness is form." But while you are practicing in this dualistic way, more and more you will have oneness with your goal. And when your practice becomes effortless, you can stop your mind. This is the stage of "form is form and emptiness is emptiness."

To stop your mind does not mean to stop the activities of mind. It means your mind pervades your whole body. Your mind follows your breathing. With your full mind you form the mudra in your hands. With your whole mind you sit with painful legs without being disturbed by them.

This is to sit without any gaining idea. At first you feel some restriction in your posture, but when you are not disturbed by the restriction, you have found the meaning of "emptiness is emptiness and form is form." So to find your own way under some restriction is the way of practice.

Practice does not mean that whatever you do, even lying down, is zazen. When the restrictions you have do not limit you, this is what we mean by practice. When you say, "Whatever I do is Buddha nature, so it doesn't matter what I do, and there is no need to practice zazen," that is already a dualistic understanding of our everyday life. If it really does not matter, there is no need for you even to say so. As long as you are concerned about what you do, that is dualistic. If you are not concerned about what you do, you will not say so. When you sit, you will sit. When you eat, you will eat. That is all. If you say, "It doesn't matter," it means that you are making some excuse to do something in your own way with your small mind. It means you are attached to some particular thing or way. That is not what we mean when we say, "Just to sit is enough," or "Whatever you do is zazen." Of course whatever we do *is* zazen, but if so, there is no need to say it.

When you sit, you should just sit without being disturbed by your painful legs or sleepiness. That is zazen. But at first it is very difficult to accept things as they are. You will be annoyed by the feeling you have in your practice. When you can do everything, whether it is good or bad, without disturbance or without being annoyed by the feeling, that is actually what we mean by "form is form and emptiness is emptiness."

When you suffer from an illness like cancer, and you realize you cannot live more than two or three years, then seeking something upon which to rely, you may start practice. One person may rely on the help of God. Someone else may start the practice of zazen. His practice will be concentrated on obtaining emptiness of mind. That means he is trying to be free from the suffering of duality. This is the practice of "form is emptiness and emptiness is form." Because of the truth of emptiness, he wants to have the actual realization of it in his life. If he practices in this way, believing and making an effort, it will help him, of course, but it is not perfect practice.

Knowing that your life is short, to enjoy it day after day, moment after moment, is the life of "form is form and emptiness is emptiness." When Buddha comes, you will welcome him; when the devil comes, you will welcome him. The famous Chinese Zen master Baso said, "Sun-faced Buddha and moon-faced Buddha." When he was ill, someone asked him, "How are you?" And he answered, "Sun-faced Buddha and moon-faced Buddha." That is the life of "form is form and emptiness is emptiness." There is no problem. One year of life is good. One hundred years of life are good. If you continue our practice, you will attain this stage.

At first you will have various problems, and it is necessary for you to make some effort to continue our practice. For the beginner, practice without effort is not true practice. For the beginner, the practice needs great effort. Especially for young people, it is necessary to try very hard to achieve something. You must stretch out your arms and legs as wide as they will go. Form is form. You must be true to your own way until at last you actually come to the point where you see it is necessary to forget all about yourself. Until you come to this point, it is completely mistaken to think that whatever you do is Zen or that it does not matter whether you practice or not. But if you make your best effort just to continue your practice with your whole mind and body, without gaining ideas, then whatever you do will be true practice. Just to continue should be your purpose. When you do something, just to do it should be your purpose. Form is form and you are you, and true emptiness will be realized in your practice.

B OWING   *"Bowing is a very serious practice. You should be prepared to bow, even in your last moment. Even though it is impossible to get rid of our self-centered desires, we have to do it. Our true nature wants us to."*

After zazen we bow to the floor nine times. By bowing we are giving up ourselves. To give up ourselves means to give up our dualistic ideas. So there is no difference between zazen practice and bowing. Usually to bow means to pay our respects to something which is more worthy of respect than ourselves. But when you bow to Buddha you should have no idea of Buddha, you just become one with Buddha, you are already Buddha himself. When you become one with Buddha, one with everything that exists, you find the true meaning of being. When you forget all your dualistic ideas, everything becomes your teacher, and everything can be the object of worship.

When everything exists within your big mind, all dualistic relationships drop away. There is no distinction between heaven and earth, man and woman, teacher and disciple. Sometimes a man bows to a woman; sometimes a woman bows to a man. Sometimes the disciple bows to the master; sometimes the master bows to the disciple. A master who cannot bow to his disciple cannot bow to Buddha. Sometimes the master and disciple bow together to Buddha. Sometimes we may bow to cats and dogs.

In your big mind, everything has the same value. Everything is Buddha himself. You see something or hear a sound, and there you have everything just as it is. In your practice you should accept everything as it is, giving to each thing the same respect given to a Buddha. Here there is Buddhahood. Then Buddha bows to Buddha, and you bow to yourself. This is the true bow.

If you do not have this firm conviction of big mind in your practice, your bow will be dualistic. When you are just yourself, you bow to yourself in its true sense, and you are one with everything. Only when you are you yourself can you bow to everything in its true sense. Bowing is a very serious practice. You should be prepared to bow even in your last moment; when you cannot do anything except bow, you should do it. This kind of conviction is necessary. Bow with this spirit and all the precepts, all the teachings are yours, and you will possess everything within your big mind.

Sen no Rikyu, the founder of the Japanese tea ceremony, committed *hara-kiri* (ritual suicide by disembowelment) in 1591 at the order of his lord, Hideyoshi. Just before Rikyu took his own life he said, "When I have this sword there is no Buddha and no Patriarchs." He meant that when we have the sword of big mind, there is no dualistic world. The only thing which exists is this spirit. This kind of imperturbable spirit was always present in Rikyu's tea ceremony. He never did anything in just a dualistic way; he was ready to die in each moment. In ceremony after ceremony he died, and he renewed himself. This is the spirit of the tea ceremony. This is how we bow.

My teacher had a callus on his forehead from bowing. He knew he was an obstinate, stubborn fellow, and so he bowed and bowed and bowed. The reason he bowed was that inside himself he always heard his master's scolding voice. He had joined the Soto order when he was thirty, which for a Japanese priest is rather late. When we are young we are less stubborn, and it is easier to get rid of our selfishness. So his master always called my teacher "You-lately-joined-fellow," and scolded him for joining so late. Actually his master loved him for his stubborn character. When my teacher was seventy, he said, "When I was young I was like a tiger, but now I am like a cat!" He was very pleased to be like a cat.

Bowing helps to eliminate our self-centered ideas. This is not so easy. It is difficult to get rid of these ideas, and bowing is a very valuable practice. The result is not the point; it is the effort to improve ourselves that is valuable. There is no end to this practice.

Each bow expresses one of the four Buddhist vows. These vows are: "Although sentient beings are innumerable, we vow to save them. Although our evil desires are limitless, we vow to be rid of them. Although the teaching is limitless, we vow to learn it all. Although Buddhism is unattainable, we vow to attain it." If it is unattainable, how can we attain it? But we should! That is Buddhism.

To think, "Because it is possible we will do it," is not Buddhism. Even though it is impossible, we have to do it because our true nature wants us to. But actually, whether or not it is possible is not the point. If it is our inmost desire to get rid of our self-centered ideas, we have to do it. When we make this effort, our inmost desire is appeased and Nirvana is there. Before you determine to do it, you have difficulty, but once you start to do it, you have none. Your effort appeases your inmost desire. There is no other way to attain calmness. Calmness of mind does not mean you should stop your activity. Real calmness should be found in activity itself. We say, "It is easy to have calmness in inactivity, it is hard to have calmness in activity, but calmness in activity is true calmness."

After you have practiced for a while, you will realize that it is not possible to make rapid, extraordinary progress. Even though you try very hard, the progress you make is always little by little. It is not like going out in a shower in which you know when you get wet. In a fog, you do not know you are getting wet, but as you keep walking you get wet little by little. If your mind has ideas of progress, you may say, "Oh, this pace is terrible!" But actually it is not. When you get wet in a fog it is very difficult to dry yourself. So there is no need to worry about progress. It is like studying a foreign language; you cannot do it all of a sudden, but by repeating it over and over you will master it. This is the Soto way of practice. We can say either that we make progress little by little, or that we do not even expect to make progress. Just to be sincere and make our full effort in each moment is enough. There is no Nirvana outside our practice.

NOTHING SPECIAL

"If you continue this simple practice every day, you will obtain some wonderful power. Before you attain it, it is something wonderful, but after you attain it, it is nothing special."

I do not feel like speaking after zazen. I feel the practice of zazen is enough. But if I must say something I think I would like to talk about how wonderful it is to practice zazen. Our purpose is just to keep this practice forever. This practice started from beginningless time, and it will continue into an endless future. Strictly speaking, for a human being there is no other practice than this practice. There is no other way of life than this way of life. Zen practice is the direct expression of our true nature.

Of course, whatever we do is the expression of our true nature, but without this practice it is difficult to realize. It is our human nature to be active and the nature of every existence. As long as we are alive, we are always doing something. But as long as you think, "I am doing this," or "I have to do this," or "I must attain something special," you are actually not doing anything. When you give up, when you no longer want something, or when you do not try to do anything special, then you do something. When there is no gaining idea in what you do, then you do something. In zazen what you are doing is not for the sake of anything. You may feel as if you are doing something special, but actually it is only the expression of your true nature; it is the activity which appeases your inmost desire. But as long as you think you are practicing zazen for the sake of something, that is not true practice.

If you continue this simple practice every day you will obtain a wonderful power. Before you attain it, it is something wonderful, but after you obtain it, it is nothing special. It is just you yourself, nothing special. As a Chinese poem says, "I went and I returned. It was nothing special. Rozan famous for its misty mountains; Sekko for its water." People think it must be wonderful to see the famous range of mountains covered by mists, and the water said to cover all the earth. But if you go there you will just see water and mountains. Nothing special. _So true!_

It is a kind of mystery that for people who have no experience of enlightenment, enlightenment is something wonderful. But if they attain it, it is nothing. But yet it is not nothing. Do you understand? For a mother with children, having children is nothing special. That is zazen. So, if you continue this practice, more and more you will acquire something—nothing special, but nevertheless something. You may say "universal nature" or "Buddha nature" or "enlightenment." You may call it by many names, but for the person who has it, it is nothing, and it is something.

When we express our true nature, we are human beings. When we do not, we do not know what we are. We are not an animal, because we walk on two legs. We are something different from an animal, but what are we? We may be a ghost; we do not know what to call ourselves. Such a creature does not actually exist. It is a delusion. We are not a human being anymore, but we do exist. When Zen is not Zen, nothing exists. Intellectually my talk makes no sense, but if you have experienced true practice, you will understand what I mean. If something exists, it has its own true nature, its Buddha nature. In the Parinirvana Sutra, Buddha says, "Everything has Buddha nature," but Dogen reads it in this way: "Everything _is_ Buddha nature." There is a difference. If you say, "Everything has Buddha nature," it means Buddha nature is in each existence, so Buddha nature and each existence are different. But when you say, "Everything *is* Buddha nature," it means everything is Buddha nature itself. When there is no Buddha nature, there is nothing at all. Something apart from Buddha nature is just a delusion. It may exist in your mind, but such things actually do not exist.

So to be a human being is to be a Buddha. Buddha nature is just another name for human nature, our true human nature. Thus even though you do not do anything, you are actually doing something. You are expressing yourself. You are expressing your true nature. Your eyes will express; your voice will express; your demeanor will express. The most important thing is to express your true nature in the simplest, most adequate way and to appreciate it in the smallest existence.

While you are continuing this practice, week after week, year after year, your experience will become deeper and deeper, and your experience will cover everything you do in your everyday life. The most important thing is to forget all gaining ideas, all dualistic ideas. In other words, just practice zazen in a certain posture. Do not think about anything. Just remain on your cushion without expecting anything. Then eventually you will resume your own true nature. That is to say, your own true nature resumes itself.

PART TWO

Right Attitude

The point we emphasize is strong confidence in our original nature.

S INGLE-MINDED WAY   *"Even if the sun were to rise from the west, the Bodhisattva has only one way."*

The purpose of my talk is not to give you some intellectual understanding, but just to express my appreciation of our Zen practice. To be able to sit with you in zazen is very, very unusual. Of course, whatever we do is unusual, because our life itself is so unusual. Buddha said, "To appreciate your human life is as rare as soil on your fingernail." You know, dirt hardly ever sticks on your nail. Our human life is rare and wonderful; when I sit I want to remain sitting forever, but I encourage myself to have another practice, for instance to recite the sutra, or to bow. And when I bow, I think, "This is wonderful." But I have to change my practice again to recite the sutra. So the purpose of my talk is to express my appreciation, that is all. Our way is not to sit to acquire something; it is to express our true nature. That is our practice.

If you want to express yourself, your true nature, there should be some natural and appropriate way of expression. Even swaying right and left as you sit down or get up from zazen is an expression of yourself. It is not preparation for practice, or relaxation after practice; it is part of the practice. So we should not do it as if it were preparing for something else. This should be true in your everyday life. To cook, or to fix some food, is not preparation, according to Dogen; it is practice. To cook is not just to prepare food for someone or for yourself; it is to express your sincerity. So when you cook you should express yourself in your activity in the kitchen. You should allow yourself plenty of time; you should work on it with nothing in your mind, and without expecting anything. You should just cook! That is also an expression of our sincerity, a part of our practice. It is necessary to sit in zazen, in this way, but sitting is not our only way. Whatever you do, it should be an expression of the same deep activity. We should appreciate what we are doing. There is no preparation for something else.

The Bodhisattva's way is called "the single-minded way," or "one railway track thousands of miles long." The railway track is always the same. If it were to become wider or narrower, it would be disastrous. Wherever you go, the railway track is always the same. That is the Bodhisattva's way. So even if the sun were to rise from the west, the Bodhisattva has only one way. His way is in each moment to express his nature and his sincerity.

We say "railway track," but actually there is no such thing. Sincerity itself is the railway track. The sights we see from the train will change, but we are always running on the same track. And there is no beginning or end to the track: beginningless and endless track. There is no starting point, no goal, nothing to attain. Just to run on the track is our way. This is the nature of our Zen practice.

But when you become curious about the railway track, danger is there. You should not see the railway track. If you look at the track you will become dizzy. Just appreciate the sights you see from the train. That is our way. There is no need for the passengers to be curious about the track. Someone will take care of it; Buddha will take care of it. But sometimes we try to explain the railway track because we become curious if something is always the same. We wonder, "How is it possible for the Bodhisattva always to be the same? What is his secret?" But there is no secret. Everyone has the same nature as the railway track.

There were two good friends, Chokei and Hofuku. They were talking about the Bodhisattva's way, and Chokei said, "Even if the arhat (an enlightened one) were to have evil desires, still the Tathagata (Buddha) does not have two kinds of words. I say that the Tathagata has words, but no dualistic words." Hofuku said, "Even though you say so, your comment is not perfect." Chokei asked, "What is your understanding of the Tathagata's words?" Hofuku said, "We have had enough discussion, so let's have a cup of tea!" Hofuku did not give his friend an answer, because it is impossible to give a verbal interpretation of our way. Nevertheless, as a part of their practice these two good friends discussed the Bodhisattva's way, even though they did not expect to find a new interpretation. So Hofuku answered, "Our discussion is over. Let's have a cup of tea!"

That is a very good answer, isn't it? It is the same for my talk—when my talk is over, your listening is over. There is no need to remember what I say; there is no need to understand what I say. You understand; you have full understanding within yourself. There is no problem.

REPETITION   *"If you lose the spirit of repetition, your practice will become quite difficult."*

The Indian thought and practice encountered by Buddha was based on an idea of human beings as a combination of spiritual and physical elements. They thought that the physical side of man bound the spiritual side, and so their religious practice was aimed at making the physical element weaker in order to free and strengthen the spirit. Thus the practice Buddha found in India emphasized asceticism. But Buddha found when he practiced asceticism that there was no limit to the attempt to purge ourselves physically, and that it made religious practice very idealistic. This kind of war with our body can only end when we die. But according to this Indian thought, we will return in another life, and another life, to repeat the struggle over and over again, without ever attaining perfect enlightenment. And even if you think you can make your physical strength weak enough to free your spiritual power, it will only work as long as you continue your ascetic practice. If you resume your everyday life you will have to strengthen your body, but then you will have to weaken it again to regain your spiritual power. And then you will have to repeat this process over and over again. This may be too great a simplification of the Indian practice encountered by Buddha, and we may laugh at it, but actually some people continue this practice even today. Sometimes without realizing it, this idea of asceticism is in the back of their minds. But practicing in this way will not result in any progress.

Buddha's way was quite different. At first he studied the Hindu practice of his time and area, and he practiced asceticism. But Buddha was not interested in the elements comprising human beings, nor in metaphysical theories of existence. He was more concerned about how he himself existed in this moment. That was his point. Bread is made from flour. How flour becomes bread when put in the oven was for Buddha the most important thing. How we become enlightened was his main interest. The enlightened person is some perfect, desirable character, for himself and for others. Buddha wanted to find out how human beings develop this ideal character—how various sages in the past became sages. In order to find out how dough became perfect bread, he made it over and over again, until he became quite successful. That was his practice.

But we may find it not so interesting to cook the same thing over and over again every day. It is rather tedious, you may say. If you lose the spirit of repetition it will become quite difficult, but it will not be difficult if you are full of strength and vitality. Anyway, we cannot keep still; we have to do something. So if you do something, you should be very observant, and careful, and alert. Our way is to put the dough in the oven and watch it carefully. Once you know how the dough becomes bread, you will understand enlightenment. So how this physical body becomes a sage is our main interest. We are not so concerned about what flour is, or what dough is, or what a sage is. A sage is a sage. Metaphysical explanations of human nature are not the point.

So the kind of practice we stress thus cannot become too idealistic. If an artist becomes too idealistic, he will commit suicide, because between his ideal and his actual ability there is a great gap. Because there is no bridge long enough to go across the gap, he will begin to despair. That is the usual spiritual way. But our spiritual way is not so idealistic. In some sense we should be idealistic; at least we should be interested in making bread which tastes and looks good! Actual practice is repeating over and over again until you find out how to become bread. There is no secret in our way. Just to practice zazen and put ourselves into the oven is our way.

Z EN AND EXCITEMENT   *"Zen is not some kind of excitement, but concentration on our usual everyday routine."*

My master died when I was thirty-one. Although I wanted to devote myself just to Zen practice at Eiheiji monastery, I had to succeed my master at his temple. I became quite busy, and being so young I had many difficulties. These difficulties gave me some experience, but it meant nothing compared with the true, calm, serene way of life.

It is necessary for us to keep the constant way. Zen is not some kind of excitement, but concentration on our usual everyday routine. If you become too busy and too excited, your mind becomes rough and ragged. This is not good. If possible, try to be always calm and joyful and keep yourself from excitement. Usually we become busier and busier, day by day, year by year, especially in our modern world. If we revisit old, familiar places after a long time, we are astonished by the changes. It cannot be helped. But if we become interested in some excitement, or in our own change, we will become completely involved in our busy life, and we will be lost. But if your mind is calm and constant, you can keep yourself away from the noisy world even though you are in the midst of it. In the midst of noise and change, your mind will be quiet and stable.

Zen is not something to get excited about. Some people start to practice Zen just out of curiosity, and they only make themselves busier. If your practice makes you worse, it is ridiculous. I think that if you try to do zazen once a week, that will make you busy enough. Do not be too interested in Zen. When young people get excited about Zen they often give up schooling and go to some mountain or forest in order to sit. That kind of interest is not true interest.

Just continue in your calm, ordinary practice and your character will be built up. If your mind is always busy, there will be no time to build, and you will not be successful, particularly if you work too hard on it. Building character is like making bread—you have to mix it little by little, step by step, and moderate temperature is needed. You know yourself quite well, and you know how much temperature you need. You know exactly what you need. But if you get too excited, you will forget how much temperature is good for you, and you will lose your own way. This is very dangerous.

Buddha said the same thing about the good ox driver. The driver knows how much load the ox can carry, and he keeps the ox from being overloaded. You know your way and your state of mind. Do not carry too much! Buddha also said that building character is like building a dam. You should be very careful in making the bank. If you try to do it all at once, water will leak from it. Make the bank carefully and you will end up with a fine dam for the reservoir.

Our unexciting way of practice may appear to be very negative. This is not so. It is a wise and effective way to work on ourselves. It is just very plain. I find this point very difficult for people, especially young people, to understand. On the other hand it may seem as if I am speaking about gradual attainment. This is not so either. In fact, this is the sudden way, because when your practice is calm and ordinary, everyday life itself is enlightenment.

R IGHT EFFORT *"If your practice is good, you may become proud of it. What you do is good, but something more is added to it. Pride is extra. Right effort is to get rid of something extra."*

The most important point in our practice is to have right or perfect effort. Right effort directed in the right direction is necessary. If your effort is headed in the wrong direction, especially if you are not aware of this, it is deluded effort. Our effort in our practice should be directed from achievement to non-achievement.

Usually when you do something, you want to achieve something, you attach to some result. From achievement to non-achievement means to be rid of the unnecessary and bad results of effort. If you do something in the spirit of non-achievement, there is a good quality in it. So just to do something without any particular effort is enough. When you make some special effort to achieve something, some excessive quality, some extra element is involved in it. You should get rid of excessive things. If your practice is good, without being aware of it you will become proud of your practice. That pride is extra. What you do is good, but something more is added to it. So you should get rid of that something which is extra. This point is very, very important, but usually we are not subtle enough to realize it, and we go in the wrong direction.

Because all of us are doing the same thing, making the same mistake, we do not realize it. So without realizing it, we are making many mistakes. And we create problems among us. This kind of bad effort is called being "Dharma-ridden," or "practice-ridden." You are involved in some idea of practice or attainment, and you cannot get out of it. When you are involved in some dualistic idea, it means your practice is not pure. By purity we do not mean to polish something, trying to make some impure thing pure. By purity we just mean things as they are. When something is added, that is impure. When something becomes dualistic, that is not pure. If you think you will get something from practicing zazen, already you are involved in impure practice. It is all right to say there is practice, and there is enlightenment, but we should not be caught by the statement. You should not be tainted by it. When you practice zazen, just practice zazen. If enlightenment comes, it just comes. We should not attach to the attainment. The true quality of zazen is always there, even if you are not aware of it, so forget all about what you think you may have gained from it. Just do it. The quality of zazen will express itself; then you will have it.

People ask what it means to practice zazen with no gaining idea, what kind of effort is necessary for that kind of practice. The answer is: effort to get rid of something extra from our practice. If some extra idea comes, you should try to stop it; you should remain in pure practice. That is the point towards which our effort is directed.

We say, "To hear the sound of one hand clapping." Usually the sound of clapping is made with two hands, and we think that clapping with one hand makes no sound at all. But actually, one hand *is* sound. Even though you do not hear it, there is sound. If you clap with two hands, you can hear the sound. But if sound did not already exist before you clapped, you could not make the sound. Before you make it there is sound. Because there is sound, you can make it, and you can hear it. Sound is everywhere. If you just practice it, there is sound. Do not try to listen to it. If you do not listen to it, the sound is all over. Because you try to hear it, sometimes there is sound, and sometimes there is no sound. Do you understand? Even though you do not do anything, you have the quality of zazen always. But if you try to find it, if you try to see the quality, you have no quality.

You are living in this world as one individual, but before you take the form of a human being, you are already there, always there. We are always here. Do you understand? You think before you were born you were not here. But how is it possible for you to appear in this world, when there is no you? Because you are already there, you can appear in the world. Also, it is not possible for something to vanish which does not exist. Because something is there, something can vanish. You may think that when you die, you disappear, you no longer exist. But even though you vanish, something which is existent cannot be non-existent. That is the magic. We ourselves cannot put any magic spells on this world. The world is its own magic. If we are looking at something, it can vanish from our sight, but if we do not try to see it, that something cannot vanish. Because you are watching it, it can disappear, but if no one is watching, how is it possible for anything to disappear? If someone is watching you, you can escape from him, but if no one is watching, you cannot escape from yourself.

So try not to see something in particular; try not to achieve anything special. You already have everything in your own pure quality. If you understand this ultimate fact, there is no fear. There may be some difficulty, of course, but there is no fear. If people have difficulty without being aware of the difficulty, that is true difficulty. They may appear very confident, they may think they are making a big effort in the right direction, but without knowing it, what they do comes out of fear. Something may vanish for them. But if your effort is in the right direction, then there is no fear of losing anything. Even if it is in the wrong direction, if you are aware of that, you will not be deluded. There is nothing to lose. There is only the constant pure quality of right practice.

N O TRACE *"When you do something, you should burn yourself completely, like a good bonfire, leaving no trace of yourself."*

When we practice zazen our mind is calm and quite simple. But usually our mind is very busy and complicated, and it is difficult to be concentrated on what we are doing. This is because before we act we think, and this thinking leaves some trace. Our activity is shadowed by some preconceived idea. The thinking not only leaves some trace or shadow, but also gives us many other notions about other activities and things. These traces and notions make our minds very complicated. When we do something with a quite simple, clear mind, we have no notion or shadows, and our activity is strong and straightforward. But when we do something with a complicated mind, in relation to other things or people, or society, our activity becomes very complex.

Most people have a double or triple notion in one activity. There is a saying, "To catch two birds with one stone." That is what people usually try to do. Because they want to catch too many birds they find it difficult to be concentrated on one activity, and they may end up not catching any birds at all! That kind of thinking always leaves its shadow on their activity. The shadow is not actually the thinking itself. Of course it is often necessary to think or prepare before we act. But right thinking does not leave any shadow. Thinking which leaves traces comes out of your relative confused mind. Relative mind is the mind which sets itself in relation to other things, thus limiting itself. It is this small mind which creates gaining ideas and leaves traces of itself.

If you leave a trace of your thinking on your activity, you will be attached to the trace. For instance, you may say, "This is what I have done!" But actually it is not so. In your recollection you may say, "I did such and such a thing in some certain way," but actually that is never exactly what happened. When you think in this way you limit the actual experience of what you have done. So if you attach to the idea of what you have done, you are involved in selfish ideas.

Often we think what we have done is good, but it may not actually be so. When we become old, we are often very proud of what we have done. When others listen to someone proudly telling something which he has done, they will feel funny, because they know his recollection is one-sided. They know that what he has told them is not exactly what he did. Moreover, if he is proud of what he did, that pride will create some problem for him. Repeating his recollections in this way, his personality will be twisted more and more, until he becomes quite a disagreeable, stubborn fellow. This is an example of leaving a trace of one's thinking. We should not forget what we did, but it should be without an extra trace. To leave a trace is not the same as to remember something. It is necessary to remember what we have done, but we should not become attached to what we have done in some special sense. What we call "attachment" is just these traces of our thought and activity.

In order not to leave any traces, when you do something, you should do it with your whole body and mind; you should be concentrated on what you do. You should do it completely, like a good bonfire. You should not be a smoky fire. You should burn yourself completely. If you do not burn yourself completely, a trace of yourself will be left in what you do. You will have something remaining which is not completely burned out. Zen activity is activity which is completely burned out, with nothing remaining but ashes. This is the goal of our practice. That is what Dogen meant when he said, "Ashes do not come back to firewood." Ash is ash. Ash should be completely ash. The firewood should be firewood. When this kind of activity takes place, one activity covers everything.

So our practice is not a matter of one hour or two hours, or one day or one year. If you practice zazen with your whole body and mind, even for a moment, that is zazen. So moment after moment you should devote yourself to your practice. You should not have any remains after you do something. But this does not mean to forget all about it. If you understand this point, all the dualistic thinking and all the problems of life will vanish.

When you practice Zen you become one with Zen. There is no you and no zazen. When you bow, there is no Buddha and no you. One complete bowing takes place, that is all. This is Nirvana. When Buddha transmitted our practice to Maha Kashyapa, he just picked up a flower with a smile. Only Maha Kashyapa understood what he meant; no one else understood. We do not know if this is a historical event or not, but it means something. It is a demonstration of our traditional way. Some activity which covers everything is true activity, and the secret of this activity is transmitted from Buddha to us. This is Zen practice, not some teaching taught by Buddha, or some rules of life set up by him. The teaching or the rules should be changed according to the place, or according to the people who observe them, but the secret of this practice cannot be changed. It is always true.

So for us there is no other way to live in this world. I think this is quite true; and this is easy to accept, easy to understand, and easy to practice. If you compare the kind of life based on this practice with what is happening in this world, or in human society, you will find out just how valuable the truth Buddha left us is. It is quite simple, and practice is quite simple. But even so, we should not ignore it; its great value must be discovered. Usually when it is so simple we say, "Oh, I know that! It is quite simple. Everyone knows that." But if we do not find its value, it means nothing. It is the same as not knowing. The more you understand culture, the more you will understand how true and how necessary this teaching is. Instead of only criticizing your culture, you should devote your mind and body to practicing this simple way. Then society and culture will grow out of you. It may be all right for the people who are too attached to their culture to be critical. Their critical attitude means they are coming back to the simple truth left by Buddha. But our approach is just to be concentrated on a simple basic practice and a simple basic understanding of life. There should be no traces in our activity. We should not attach to some fancy ideas or to some beautiful things. We should not seek for something good. The truth is always near at hand, within your reach.

GOD GIVING

"'To give is nonattachment,' that is, just not to attach to anything is to give."

Every existence in nature, every existence in the human world, every cultural work that we create, is something which was given, or is being given to us, relatively speaking. But as everything is originally one, we are, in actuality, giving out everything. Moment after moment we are creating something, and this is the joy of our life. But this "I" which is creating and always giving out something is not the "small I"; it is the "big I." Even though you do not realize the oneness of this "big I" with everything, when you give something you feel good, because at that time you feel at one with what you are giving. This is why it feels better to give than to take.

We have a saying, *"Dana prajna paramita." Dana* means to give, *prajna* is wisdom, and *paramita* means to cross over, or to reach the other shore. Our life can be seen as a crossing of a river. The goal of our life's effort is to reach the other shore, Nirvana. *Prajna paramita,* the true wisdom of life, is that in each step of the way, the other shore is actually reached. To reach the other shore with each step of the crossing is the way of true living. *Dana prajna paramita* is the first of the six ways of true living. The second is *sila prajna paramita,* or the Buddhist precepts. Then there are *kshanti prajna paramita,* or endurance; *virya prajna paramita,* or ardor and constant effort; *dhyana prajna paramita,* or Zen practice; and *prajna paramita,* or wisdom. Actually these six *prajna paramita* are one, but as we can observe life from various sides, we count six.

Dogen-zenji said, "To give is nonattachment." That is,

just not to attach to anything is to give. It does not matter what is given. To give a penny or a piece of leaf is *dana prajna paramita*; to give one line, or even one word of teaching is *dana prajna paramita*. If given in the spirit of nonattachment, the material offering and the teaching offering have the same value. With the right spirit, all that we do, all that we create is *dana prajna paramita*. So Dogen said, "To produce something, to participate in human activity is also *dana prajna paramita*. To provide a ferryboat for people, or to make a bridge for people is *dana prajna paramita*." Actually, to give one line of the teaching may be to make a ferryboat for someone!

According to Christianity, every existence in nature is something which was created for or given to us by God. That is the perfect idea of giving. But if you think that God created man, and that you are somehow separate from God, you are liable to think you have the ability to create something separate, something not given by Him. For instance, we create airplanes and highways. And when we repeat, "I create, I create, I create," soon we forget who is actually the "I" which creates the various things; we soon forget about God. This is the danger of human culture. Actually, to create with the "big I" is to give; we cannot create and own what we create for ourselves since everything was created by God. This point should not be forgotten. But because we do forget who is doing the creating and the reason for the creation, we become attached to the material or exchange value. This has no value in comparison to the absolute value of something as God's creation. Even though something has no material or relative value to any "small I," it has absolute value in itself. Not to be attached to something is to be aware of its absolute value. Everything you do should be based on such an awareness, and not on material or self-centered ideas of value. Then whatever you do is true giving, is *dana prajna paramita.*

When we sit in the cross-legged posture, we resume our fundamental activity of creation. There are perhaps three kinds of creation. The first is to be aware of ourselves after we finish zazen. When we sit we are nothing, we do not even realize what we are; we just sit. But when we stand up, we are there! That is the first step in creation. When you are there, everything else is there; everything is created all at once. When we emerge from nothing, when everything emerges from nothing, we see it all as a fresh new creation. This is nonattachment. The second kind of creation is when you act, or produce or prepare something like food or tea. The third kind is to create something within yourself, such as education, or culture, or art, or some system for our society. So there are three kinds of creation. But if you forget the first, the most important one, the other two will be like children who have lost their parents; their creation will mean nothing.

Usually everyone forgets about zazen. Everyone forgets about God. They work very hard at the second and third kinds of creation, but God does not help the activity. How is it possible for Him to help when He does not realize who He is? That is why we have so many problems in this world. When we forget the fundamental source of our creating, we are like children who do not know what to do when they lose their parents.

If you understand *dana prajna paramita,* you will understand how it is we create so many problems for ourselves. Of course, to live is to create problems. If we did not appear in this world, our parents would have no difficulty

with us! Just by appearing we create problems for them. This is all right. Everything creates some problems. But usually people think that when they die, everything is over, the problems disappear. But your death may create problems too! Actually, our problems should be solved or dissolved in this life. But if we are aware that what we do or what we create is really the gift of the "big I," then we will not be attached to it, and we will not create problems for ourselves or for others.

And we should forget, day by day, what we have done; this is true nonattachment. And we should do something new. To do something new, of course we must know our past, and this is all right. But we should not keep holding on to anything we have done; we should only reflect on it. And we must have some idea of what we should do in the future. But the future is the future, the past is the past; now we should work on something new. This is our attitude, and how we should live in this world. This is *dana prajna paramita,* to give something, or to create something for ourselves. So to do something through and through is to resume our true activity of creation. This is why we sit. If we do not forget this point, everything will be carried on beautifully. But once we forget this point, the world will be filled with confusion.

MISTAKES IN PRACTICE

"It is when your practice is rather greedy that you become discouraged with it. So you should be grateful that you have a sign or warning signal to show you the weak point in your practice."

There are several poor ways of practice that you should understand. Usually when you practice zazen, you become very idealistic, and you set up an ideal or goal which you strive to attain and fulfill. But as I have often said, this is absurd. When you are idealistic, you have some gaining idea within yourself; by the time you attain your ideal or goal, your gaining idea will create another ideal. So as long as your practice is based on a gaining idea, and you practice zazen in an idealistic way, you will have no time actually to attain your ideal. Moreover, you will be sacrificing the meat of your practice. Because your attainment is always ahead, you will always be sacrificing yourself now for some ideal in the future. You end up with nothing. This is absurd; it is not adequate practice at all. But even worse than this idealistic attitude is to practice zazen in competition with someone else. This is a poor, shabby kind of practice.

Our Soto way puts an emphasis on *shikan taza,* or "just sitting." Actually we do not have any particular name for our practice; when we practice zazen we just practice it, and whether we find joy in our practice or not, we just do it. Even though we are sleepy, and we are tired of practicing zazen, of repeating the same thing day after day; even so, we continue our practice. Whether or not someone encourages our practice, we just do it.

Even when you practice zazen alone, without a teacher, I

think you will find some way to tell whether your practice is adequate or not. When you are tired of sitting, or when you are disgusted with your practice, you should recognize this as a warning signal. You become discouraged with your practice when your practice has been idealistic. You have some gaining idea in your practice, and it is not pure enough. It is when your practice is rather greedy that you become discouraged with it. So you should be grateful that you have a sign or warning signal to show you the weak point in your practice. At that time, forgetting all about your mistake and renewing your way, you can resume your original practice. This is a very important point.

So as long as you continue your practice, you are quite safe, but as it is very difficult to continue, you must find some way to encourage yourself. As it is hard to encourage yourself without becoming involved in some poor kind of practice, to continue our pure practice by yourself may be rather difficult. This is why we have a teacher. With your teacher you will correct your practice. Of course you will have a very hard time with him, but even so, you will always be safe from wrong practice.

Most Zen Buddhist priests have had a difficult time with their masters. When they talk about the difficulties, you may think that without this kind of hardship you cannot practice zazen. But this is not true. Whether you have difficulties in your practice or not, as long as you continue it, you have pure practice in its true sense. Even when you are not aware of it, you have it. So Dogen-zenji said, "Do not think you will necessarily be aware of your own enlightenment." Whether or not you are aware of it, you have your own true enlightenment within your practice.

Another mistake will be to practice for the sake of the joy you find in it. Actually, when your practice is involved in a feeling of joy, it is not in very good shape either. Of course this is not poor practice, but compared to the true practice it is not so good. In Hinayana Buddhism, practice is classified in four ways. The best way is just to do it without having any joy in it, not even spiritual joy. This way is just to do it, forgetting your physical and mental feeling, forgetting all about yourself in your practice. This is the fourth stage, or the highest stage. The next highest stage is to have just physical joy in your practice. At this stage you find some pleasure in practice, and you will practice because of the pleasure you find in it. In the second stage you have both mental and physical joy, or good feeling. These two middle stages are stages in which you practice zazen because you feel good in your practice. The first stage is when you have no thinking and no curiosity in your practice. These four stages also apply to our Mahayana practice, and the highest is just to practice it.

If you find some difficulty in your practice, that is the warning that you have some wrong idea, so you have to be careful. But do not give up your practice; continue it, knowing your weakness. Here there is no gaining idea. Here there is no fixed idea of attainment. You do not say, "This is enlightenment," or "That is not right practice." Even in wrong practice, when you realize it and continue, there is right practice. Our practice cannot be perfect, but without being discouraged by this, we should continue it. This is the secret of practice.

And if you want to find some encouragement in your discouragement, getting tired of practice is itself the encouragement. You encourage yourself when you get tired of it. When you do not want to do it, that is the warning signal. It is like having a toothache when your teeth are not so good. When you feel some pain in your teeth, you go to the dentist. That is our way.

The cause of conflict is some fixed idea or one-sided idea. When everyone knows the value of pure practice, we will have little conflict in our world. This is the secret of our practice and Dogen-zenji's way. Dogen repeats this point in his book *Shobogenzo* (A Treasury of the True Dharma).

If you understand the cause of conflict as some fixed or one-sided idea, you can find meaning in various practices without being caught by any of them. If you do not realize this point you will be easily caught by some particular way, and you will say, "This is enlightenment! This is perfect practice. This is our way. The rest of the ways are not perfect. This is the best way." This is a big mistake. There is no particular way in true practice. You should find your own way, and you should know what kind of practice you have right now. Knowing both the advantages and disadvantages of some special practice, you can practice that special way without danger. But if you have a one-sided attitude, you will ignore the disadvantage of the practice, emphasizing only its good part. Eventually you will discover the worst side of the practice, and become discouraged when it is too late. This is silly. We should be grateful that the ancient teachers point out this mistake.

L IMITING YOUR ACTIVITY   *"Usually when someone believes in a particular religion, his attitude becomes
more and more a sharp angle pointing away from himself. In our
way the point of the angle is always towards ourselves."*

In our practice we have no particular purpose or goal, nor
any special object of worship. In this respect our practice
is somewhat different from the usual religious practices.
Joshu, a great Chinese Zen master, said, "A clay Buddha
cannot cross water; a bronze Buddha cannot get through a
furnace; a wooden Buddha cannot get through fire." Whatever it is, if your practice is directed toward some particular object, such as a clay, a bronze, or a wooden Buddha,
it will not always work. So as long as you have some particular goal in your practice, that practice will not help you
completely. It may help as long as you are directed towards
that goal, but when you resume your everyday life, it will
not work.

You may think that if there is no purpose or no goal in
our practice, we will not know what to do. But there is a
way. The way to practice without having any goal is to limit
your activity, or to be concentrated on what you are doing
in this moment. Instead of having some particular object in
mind, you should limit your activity. When your mind is
wandering about elsewhere you have no chance to express
yourself. But if you limit your activity to what you can do
just now, in this moment, then you can express fully your
true nature, which is the universal Buddha nature. This is
our way.

When we practice zazen we limit our activity to the
smallest extent. Just keeping the right posture and being

concentrated on sitting is how we express the universal nature. Then we become Buddha, and we express Buddha nature. So instead of having some object of worship, we just concentrate on the activity which we do in each moment. When you bow, you should just bow; when you sit, you should just sit; when you eat, you should just eat. If you do this, the universal nature is there. In Japanese we call it *ichigyo-zammai,* or "one-act *samadhi." Sammai* (or *samadhi*) is "concentration." *Ichigyo* is "one practice."

I think some of you who practice zazen here may believe in some other religion, but I do not mind. Our practice has nothing to do with some particular religious belief. And for you, there is no need to hesitate to practice our way, because it has nothing to do with Christianity or Shintoism or Hinduism. Our practice is for everyone. Usually when someone believes in a particular religion, his attitude becomes more and more a sharp angle pointing away from himself. But our way is not like this. In our way the point of the sharp angle is always towards ourselves, not away from ourselves. So there is no need to worry about the difference between Buddhism and the religion you may believe in.

Joshu's statement about the different Buddhas concerns those who direct their practice towards some particular Buddha. One kind of Buddha will not serve your purpose completely. You will have to throw it away sometime, or at least ignore it. But if you understand the secret of our practice, wherever you go, you yourself are "boss." No matter what the situation, you cannot neglect Buddha, because you yourself are Buddha. Only this Buddha will help you completely.

S TUDY YOURSELF   *"To have some deep feeling about Buddhism is not the point; we just do what we should do, like eating supper and going to bed. This is Buddhism."*

The purpose of studying Buddhism is not to study Buddhism, but to study ourselves. It is impossible to study ourselves without some teaching. If you want to know what water is you need science, and the scientist needs a laboratory. In the laboratory there are various ways in which to study what water is. Thus it is possible to know what kind of elements water has, the various forms it takes, and its nature. But it is impossible thereby to know water in itself. It is the same thing with us. We need some teaching, but just by studying the teaching alone, it is impossible to know what "I" in myself am. Through the teaching we may understand our human nature. But the teaching is not we ourselves; it is some explanation of ourselves. So if you are attached to the teaching, or to the teacher, that is a big mistake. The moment you meet a teacher, you should leave the teacher, and you should be independent. You need a teacher so that you can become independent. If you are not attached to him, the teacher will show you the way to yourself. You have a teacher for yourself, not for the teacher.

Rinzai, an early Chinese Zen master, analyzed how to teach his disciples in four ways. Sometimes he talked about the disciple himself; sometimes he talked about the teaching itself; sometimes he gave an interpretation of the disciple or the teaching; and finally, sometimes he did not give any instruction at all to his disciples. He knew that even without being given any instruction, a student is a student. Strictly speaking, there is no need to teach the student, because the student himself is Buddha, even though he may not be aware of it. And even though he is aware of his true nature, if he is attached to this awareness, that is already wrong. When he is not aware of it, he has everything, but when he becomes aware of it he thinks that what he is aware of is himself, which is a big mistake.

When you do not hear anything from the teacher, but just sit, this is called teaching without teaching. But sometimes this is not sufficient, so we listen to lectures and have discussions. But we should remember that the purpose of practice in a particular place is to study ourselves. To be independent, we study. Like the scientist, we have to have some means by which to study. We need a teacher because it is impossible to study ourselves by ourselves. But you should not make a mistake. You should not take what you have learned with a teacher for you yourself. The study you make with your teacher is a part of your everyday life, a part of your incessant activity. In this sense there is no difference between the practice and the activity you have in everyday life. So to find the meaning of your life in the zendo is to find the meaning of your everyday activity. To be aware of the meaning of your life, you practice zazen.

When I was at Eiheiji monastery in Japan, everyone was just doing what he should do. That is all. It is the same as waking up in the morning; we have to get up. At Eiheiji monastery, when we had to sit, we sat; when we had to bow to Buddha, we bowed to Buddha. That is all. And when we were practicing, we did not feel anything special. We did not even feel that we were leading a monastic life. For us, the monastic life was the usual life, and the people who came from the city were unusual people. When we saw them we felt, "Oh, some unusual people have come!"

But once I had left Eiheiji and been away for some time, coming back was different. I heard the various sounds of practice—the bells and the monks reciting the sutra—and I had a deep feeling. There were tears flowing out of my eyes, nose, and mouth! It is the people who are outside of the monastery who feel its atmosphere. Those who are practicing actually do not feel anything. I think this is true for everything. When we hear the sound of the pine trees on a windy day, perhaps the wind is just blowing, and the pine tree is just standing in the wind. That is all that they are doing. But the people who listen to the wind in the tree will write a poem, or will feel something unusual. That is, I think, the way everything is.

So to feel something about Buddhism is not the main point. Whether that feeling is good or bad is out of the question. We do not mind, whatever it is. Buddhism is not good or bad. We are doing what we should do. That is Buddhism. Of course some encouragement is necessary, but that encouragement is just encouragement. It is not the true purpose of practice. It is just medicine. When we become discouraged we want some medicine. When we are in good spirits we do not need any medicine. You should not mistake medicine for food. Sometimes medicine is necessary, but it should not become our food.

So, of Rinzai's four ways of practice, the perfect one is not to give a student any interpretation of himself, nor to give him any encouragement. If we think of ourselves as our bodies, the teaching then may be our clothing. Sometimes we talk about our clothing; sometimes we talk about our body. But neither body nor clothing is actually we ourselves. We ourselves are the big activity. We are just expressing the smallest particle of the big activity, that is all.

So it is all right to talk about ourselves, but actually there is no need to do so. Before we open our mouths, we are already expressing the big existence, including ourselves. So the purpose of talking about ourselves is to correct the misunderstanding we have when we are attached to any particular temporal form or color of the big activity. It is necessary to talk about what our body is and what our activity is so that we may not make any mistake about them. So to talk about ourselves is actually to forget about ourselves.

Dogen-zenji said, "To study Buddhism is to study ourselves. To study ourselves is to forget ourselves." When you become attached to a temporal expression of your true nature, it is necessary to talk about Buddhism, or else you will think the temporal expression is it. But this particular expression of it is not it. And yet at the same time it is it! For a while this is it; for the smallest particle of time, this is it. But it is not always so: the very next instant it is not so, thus this is not it. So that you will realize this fact, it is necessary to study Buddhism. But the purpose of studying Buddhism is to study ourselves and to forget ourselves. When we forget ourselves, we actually are the true activity of the big existence, or reality itself. When we realize this fact, there is no problem whatsoever in this world, and we can enjoy our life without feeling any difficulties. The purpose of our practice is to be aware of this fact.

TO POLISH A TILE

"When you become you, Zen becomes Zen. When you are you, you see things as they are, and you become one with your surroundings."

Zen stories, or *koans,* are very difficult to understand before you know what we are doing moment after moment. But if you know exactly what we are doing in each moment, you will not find *koans* so difficult. There are so many *koans.* I have often talked to you about a frog, and each time everybody laughs. But a frog is very interesting. He sits like us, too, you know. But he does not think that he is doing anything so special. When you go to a zendo and sit, you may think you are doing some special thing. While your husband or wife is sleeping, you are practicing zazen! You are doing some special thing, and your spouse is lazy! That may be your understanding of zazen. But look at the frog. A frog also sits like us, but he has no idea of zazen. Watch him. If something annoys him, he will make a face. If something comes along to eat, he will snap it up and eat, and he eats sitting. Actually that is our zazen—not any special thing.

Here is a kind of frog *koan* for you. Baso was a famous Zen master called the Horse-master. He was the disciple of Nangaku, one of the Sixth Patriarch's disciples. One day while he was studying under Nangaku, Baso was sitting, practicing zazen. He was a man of large physical build; when he talked, his tongue reached to his nose; his voice was loud; and his zazen must have been very good. Nangaku saw him sitting like a great mountain or like a frog. Nangaku asked, "What are you doing?" "I am practicing zazen," Baso replied. "Why are you practicing zazen?" "I want to attain enlightenment; I want to be a Buddha," the disciple said. Do you know what the teacher did? He picked up a tile, and he started to polish it. In Japan, after taking a tile from the kiln, we polish it to give it a beautiful finish. So Nangaku picked up a tile and started to polish it. Baso, his disciple, asked, "What are you doing?" "I want to make this tile into a jewel," Nangaku said. "How is it possible to make a tile a jewel?" Baso asked. "How is it possible to become a Buddha by practicing zazen?" Nangaku replied. "Do you want to attain Buddhahood? There is no Buddhahood besides your ordinary mind. When a cart does not go, which do you whip, the cart or the horse?" the master asked.

Nangaku's meaning here is that whatever you do, that is zazen. True zazen is beyond being in bed or sitting in the zendo. If your husband or wife is in bed, that is zazen. If you think, "I am sitting here, and my spouse is in bed," then even though you are sitting here in the cross-legged position, that is not true zazen. You should be like a frog always. That is true zazen.

Dogen-zenji commented on this *koan*. He said, "When the Horse-master becomes the Horse-master, Zen becomes Zen." When Baso becomes Baso, his zazen becomes true zazen, and Zen becomes Zen. What is true zazen? When you become you! When you are you, then no matter what you do, that is zazen. Even though you are in bed, you may not be you most of the time. Even though you are sitting in the zendo, I wonder whether you are you in the true sense.

Here is another famous *koan*. Zuikan was a Zen master who always used to address himself. "Zuikan?" he would call. And then he would answer. "Yes!" "Zuikan?" "Yes!" Of course he was living all alone in his small zendo, and of course he knew who he was, but sometimes he lost himself.

And whenever he lost himself, he would address himself, "Zuikan?" "Yes!"

If we are like a frog, we are always ourselves. But even a frog sometimes loses himself, and he makes a sour face. And if something comes along, he will snap at it and eat it. So I think a frog is always addressing himself. I think you should do that also. Even in zazen you will lose yourself. When you become sleepy, or when your mind starts to wander about, you lose yourself. When your legs become painful— "Why are my legs so painful?"—you lose yourself. Because you lose yourself, your problem will be a problem for you. If you do not lose yourself, then even though you have difficulty, there is actually no problem whatsoever. You just sit in the midst of the problem; when you are a part of the problem, or when the problem is a part of you, there *is* no problem, because you are the problem itself. The problem is you yourself. If this is so, there is no problem.

When your life is always a part of your surroundings—in other words, when you are called back to yourself, in the present moment—then there is no problem. When you start to wander about in some delusion which is something apart from you yourself, then your surroundings are not real anymore, and your mind is not real anymore. If you yourself are deluded, then your surroundings are also a misty, foggy delusion. Once you are in the midst of delusion, there is no end to delusion. You will be involved in deluded ideas one after another. Most people live in delusion, involved in their problem, trying to solve their problem. But just to live is actually to live in problems. And to solve the problem is to be a part of it, to be one with it.

So which do you hit, the cart or the horse? Which do you hit, yourself or your problems? If you start questioning which you should hit, that means you have already started to wander about. But when you actually hit the horse, the cart will go. In truth, the cart and the horse are not different. When you are you, there is no problem of whether you should hit the cart or the horse. When you are you, zazen becomes true zazen. So when you practice zazen, your problem will practice zazen, and everything else will practice zazen too. Even though your spouse is in bed, he or she is also practicing zazen—when *you* practice zazen! But when you do not practice true zazen, then there is your spouse, and there is yourself, each quite different, quite separate from the other. So if you yourself have true practice, then everything else is practicing our way at the same time.

That is why we should always address ourselves, checking up on ourselves like a doctor tapping himself. This is very important. This kind of practice should be continued moment after moment, incessantly. We say, "When the night is here, the dawn comes." It means there is no gap between the dawn and the night. Before the summer is over, autumn comes. In this way we should understand our life. We should practice with this understanding, and solve our problems in this way. Actually, just to work on the problem, if you do it with single-minded effort, is enough. You should just polish the tile; that is our practice. The purpose of practice is not to make a tile a jewel. Just continue sitting; that is practice in its true sense. It is not a matter of whether or not it is possible to attain Buddhahood, whether or not it is possible to make a tile a jewel. Just to work and live in this world with this understanding is the most important point. That is our practice. That is true zazen. So we say, "When you eat, eat!" You should eat what is there, you know. Sometimes you do not eat it. Even though you are eating, your mind is somewhere else. You do not taste what you have in your mouth. As long as you can eat when you are eating, you are all right. Do not worry a bit. It means you are you yourself.

When you are you, you see things as they are, and you become one with your surroundings. There is your true self. There you have true practice; you have the practice of a frog. He is a good example of our practice—when a frog becomes a frog, Zen becomes Zen. When you understand a frog through and through, you attain enlightenment; you are Buddha. And you are good for others, too: husband or wife or son or daughter. This is zazen!

C ONSTANCY   *"People who know the state of empti-
ness will always be able to dissolve their problems by constancy."*

The message for us today is "Cultivate your own spirit." It means not to go seeking for something outside of yourself. This is a very important point, and it is the only way to practice Zen. Of course, studying scriptures or reciting the sutra or sitting is Zen; each of these activities should be Zen. But if your effort or practice does not have the right orientation, it will not work at all. Not only will it not work, but it may spoil your pure nature. Then the more you know about Zen, the more you will become spoiled. Your mind will be filled with rubbish; your mind will be stained.

It is quite usual for us to gather pieces of information from various sources, thinking in this way to increase our knowledge. Actually, following this way we end up not knowing anything at all. Our understanding of Buddhism should not be just gathering many pieces of information, seeking to gain knowledge. Instead of gathering knowledge, you should clear your mind. If your mind is clear, true knowledge is already yours. When you listen to our teaching with a pure, clear mind, you can accept it as if you were hearing something which you already knew. This is called emptiness, or omnipotent self, or knowing everything. When you know everything, you are like a dark sky. Sometimes a flashing will come through the dark sky. After it passes, you forget all about it, and there is nothing left but the dark sky. The sky is never surprised when all of a sudden a thunderbolt breaks through. And when the lightning does flash, a wonderful sight may be seen. When we have emptiness we are always prepared for watching the flashing.

In China, Rozan is famous for its misty scenery. I have not been to China yet, but there must be beautiful mountains there. And to see the white clouds or mist come and go through the mountains must be a very wonderful sight. Although it is wonderful, a Chinese poem says, "Rozan is famous for its misty, rainy days, and the great river Sekko for its tide, coming and going. That is all." That is all, but it is splendid. This is how we appreciate things.

So you should accept knowledge as if you were hearing something you already knew. But this does not mean to receive various pieces of information merely as an echo of your own opinions. It means that you should not be surprised at whatever you see or hear. If you receive things just as an echo of yourself, you do not really see them, you do not fully accept them as they are. So when we say, "Rozan is famous for its misty, rainy days," it does not mean to appreciate this sight by recollecting some scenery we have seen before: "It is not so wonderful. I have seen that sight before." Or "I have painted much more beautiful paintings! Rozan is nothing!" This is not our way. If you are ready to accept things as they are, you will receive them as old friends, even though you appreciate them with new feeling.

And we should not hoard knowledge; we should be free from our knowledge. If you collect various pieces of knowledge, as a collection it may be very good, but this is not our way. We should not try to surprise people by our wonderful treasures. We should not be interested in something special. If you want to appreciate something fully, you should forget yourself. You should accept it like lightning flashing in the utter darkness of the sky.

Sometimes we think it is impossible for us to understand something unfamiliar, but actually there is nothing that is unfamiliar to us. Some people may say, "It is almost impossible to understand Buddhism because our cultural background is so different. How can we understand Oriental thought?" Of course Buddhism cannot be separated from its cultural background; this is true. But if a Japanese Buddhist comes to the United States, he is no longer a Japanese. I am living in your cultural background. I am eating nearly the same food as you eat, and I am communicating with you in your language. Even though you do not understand me completely, I want to understand you. And I may understand you better than anyone who can speak and understand English. This is true. Even if I could not understand English at all, I think I could communicate with people. There is always a possibility of understanding as long as we exist in the utter darkness of the sky, as long as we live in emptiness.

I have always said that you must be very patient if you want to understand Buddhism, but I have been seeking for a better word than patience. The usual translation of the Japanese word *nin* is "patience," but perhaps "constancy" is a better word. You must force yourself to be patient, but in constancy there is no particular effort involved—there is only the unchanging ability to accept things as they are. For people who have no idea of emptiness, this ability may appear to be patience, but patience can actually be nonacceptance. People who know, even if only intuitively, the state of emptiness always have open the possibility of accepting things as they are. They can appreciate everything. In everything they do, even though it may be very difficult, they will always be able to dissolve their problems by constancy.

Nin is the way we cultivate our own spirit. *Nin* is our way of continuous practice. We should always live in the dark empty sky. The sky is always the sky. Even though clouds and lightning come, the sky is not disturbed. Even if the flashing of enlightenment comes, our practice forgets all about it. Then it is ready for another enlightenment. It is necessary for us to have enlightenments one after another, if possible, moment after moment. This is what is called enlightenment before you attain it and after you attain it.

COMMUNICATION   *"Without any intentional, fancy way of adjusting yourself, to express yourself as you are is the most important thing."*

Communication is very important in Zen practice. Because I cannot speak your language very well, I am always seeking some way of communicating with you. I think that this kind of effort will result in something very good. We say that if you do not understand your master's words, you are not his disciple. To understand your master's words, or your master's language, is to understand your master himself. And when you understand him, you find his language is not just ordinary language, but language in its wider sense. Through your master's language, you understand more than what his words actually say.

When we say something, our subjective intention or situation is always involved. So there is no perfect word; some distortion is always present in a statement. But nevertheless, through our master's statement we have to understand objective fact itself—the ultimate fact. By ultimate fact we do not mean something eternal or something constant, we mean things as they are in each moment. You may call it "being" or "reality."

To understand reality as a direct experience is the reason we practice zazen, and the reason we study Buddhism. Through the study of Buddhism, you will understand your human nature, your intellectual faculty, and the truth present in your human activity. And you can take this human nature of yours into consideration when you seek to understand reality. But only by the actual practice of Zen can you experience reality directly and understand in their true sense the various statements made by your teacher or by Buddha. In a strict sense, it is not possible to speak about reality. Nevertheless, if you are a Zen student, you have to understand it directly through your master's words.

Your master's direct statement may not be only in words; his behavior is likewise his way of expressing himself. In Zen we put emphasis on demeanor, or behavior. By behavior we do not mean a particular way that you ought to behave, but rather the natural expression of yourself. We emphasize straightforwardness. You should be true to your feelings, and to your mind, expressing yourself without any reservations. This helps the listener to understand more easily.

When you listen to someone, you should give up all your preconceived ideas and your subjective opinions; you should just listen to him, just observe what his way is. We put very little emphasis on right and wrong or good and bad. We just see things as they are with him, and accept them. This is how we communicate with each other. Usually when you listen to some statement, you hear it as a kind of echo of yourself. You are actually listening to your own opinion. If it agrees with your opinion you may accept it, but if it does not, you will reject it or you may not even really hear it. That is one danger when you listen to someone. The other danger is to be caught by the statement. If you do not understand your master's statement in its true sense, you will easily be caught by something which is involved in your subjective opinion, or by some particular way the statement is expressed. You will take what he says only as a statement, without understanding the spirit behind the words. This kind of danger is always there.

It is difficult to have good communication between parents and children because parents always have their own intentions. Their intentions are nearly always good, but the way they speak, or the way they express themselves, is often not so free; it is usually too one-sided and not realistic. We each have our own way of expressing ourselves, and it is difficult to change that way according to the circumstances. If parents can manage to express themselves in various ways according to each situation, there will be no danger in the education of their children. This, however, is rather difficult. Even a Zen master has his own way. When Nishiari-zenji scolded his disciples, he always said, "Go away!" One of his students took him literally and left the temple! But the master did not mean to expel the student. It was just his way of expressing himself. Instead of saying, "Be careful!" he said, "Go away!" If your parents have this kind of habit, you will easily misunderstand them. This danger is always present in your everyday life. So as a listener or a disciple, it is necessary to clear your mind of these various distortions. A mind full of preconceived ideas, subjective intentions, or habits is not open to things as they are. That is why we practice zazen: to clear our mind of what is related to something else.

To be quite natural to ourselves, and also to follow what others say or do in the most appropriate way, is quite difficult. If we try to adjust ourselves intentionally in some way, it is impossible to be natural. If you try to adjust yourself in a certain way, you will lose yourself. So without any intentional, fancy way of adjusting yourself, to express yourself freely as you are is the most important thing to make yourself happy, and to make others happy. You will acquire this kind of ability by practicing zazen. Zen is not some fancy, special art of living. Our teaching is just to live, always in reality, in its exact sense. To make our effort, moment after moment, is our way. In an exact sense, the only thing we actually can study in our life is that on which we are working in each moment. We cannot even study Buddha's words. To study Buddha's words in their exact sense means to study them through some activity which you face moment after moment. So we should be concentrated with our full mind and body on what we do; and we should be faithful, subjectively and objectively, to ourselves, and especially to our feelings. Even when you do not feel so well, it is better to express how you feel without any particular attachment or intention. So you may say, "Oh, I am sorry, I do not feel well." That is enough. You should not say, "You made me so!" That is too much. You may say, "Oh, I am sorry. I am so angry with you." There is no need to say that you are not angry when you are angry. You should just say, "I am angry." That is enough.

True communication depends upon our being straightforward with one another. Zen masters are very straightforward. If you do not understand the reality directly through your master's words, he may use his staff on you. "What is it?!" he may say. Our way is very direct. But this is not actually Zen, you know. It is not our traditional way, but when we want to express it, we find it easier sometimes to express it in this way. But the best way to communicate may be just to sit without saying anything. Then you will have the full meaning of Zen. If I use my staff on you until I lose myself, or until you die, still it will not be enough. The best way is just to sit.

NEGATIVE AND POSITIVE *"Big mind is something to express, not something to figure out. Big mind is something you have, not something to seek for."*

The more you understand our thinking, the more you find it difficult to talk about it. The purpose of my talking is to give you some idea of our way, but actually, it is not something to talk about, but something to practice. The best way is just to practice without saying anything. When we talk about our way, there is apt to be some misunderstanding, because the true way always has at least two sides, the negative and the positive. When we talk about the negative side, the positive side is missing, and when we talk about the positive side, the negative side is missing. We cannot speak in a positive and a negative way at the same time. So we do not know what to say. It is almost impossible to talk about Buddhism. So not to say anything, just to practice it, is the best way. Showing one finger or drawing a round circle may be the way, or simply to bow.

If we understand this point, we will understand how to talk about Buddhism, and we will have perfect communication. To talk about something will be one of our practices, and to listen to the talk will also be practice. When we practice zazen we just practice zazen, without any gaining idea. When we talk about something we just talk about something, just the positive or the negative side, without trying to express some intellectual, one-sided idea. And we listen without trying to figure out some intellectual understanding, without trying to understand from just a one-sided view. This is how we talk about our teaching and how we listen to a talk.

The Soto way always has double meaning, positive and negative. And our way is both Hinayanistic and Mahayanistic. I always say our practice is very Hinayanistic. Actually we have Hinayana practice with Mahayana spirit—rigid formal practice with informal mind. Although our practice looks very formal, our minds are not formal. Although we practice zazen every morning in the same way, that is no reason to call this formal practice. It is your discrimination which makes it formal or informal. Inside the practice itself, there is no formal or informal. If you have Mahayana mind, something which people call formal may be informal. So we say that observing the precepts in a Hinayana way is violating the precepts in a Mahayana way. If you observe our precepts in just a formal way, you lose your Mahayana spirit. Before you understand this point, you always have a problem: whether you should observe our way literally, or whether you should not concern yourself about the formality which we have. But if you understand our way completely, there is no such problem, because whatever you do is practice. As long as you have Mahayana mind, there is no Mahayana or Hinayana practice. Even though it seems as if you are violating the precepts, you are actually observing them in their true sense. The point is whether you have big mind or small mind. In short, when you do everything without thinking about whether it is good or bad, and when you do something with your whole mind and body, then that is our way.

Dogen-zenji said, "When you say something to someone, he may not accept it, but do not try to make him understand it intellectually. Do not argue with him; just listen to his objections until he himself finds something wrong with them." This is very interesting. Try not to force your idea on someone, but rather think about it with him. If you feel you have won the discussion, that also is the wrong attitude. Try not to win in the argument; just listen to it; but it is also wrong to behave as if you had lost. Usually when we say something, we are apt to try to sell our teaching or force our idea. But between Zen students there is no special purpose in speaking or in listening. Sometimes we listen, sometimes we talk; that is all. It is like a greeting: "Good morning!" Through this kind of communication we can develop our way.

Not to say anything may be very good, but there is no reason why we should always be silent. Whatever you do, even including not-doing, that is our practice. That is an expression of big mind. So big mind is something to express, but it is not something to figure out. Big mind is something you have, not something to seek for. Big mind is something to talk about, or to express by our activity, or something to enjoy. If we do this, in our way of observing precepts there is no Hinayana way or Mahayana way. Only because you seek to gain something through rigid formal practice does it become a problem for you. But if we appreciate whatever problem we have as an expression of big mind, it is not a problem anymore. Sometimes our problem is that big mind is very complicated; sometimes big mind is too simple to figure out. That is also big mind. But because you try to figure out what it is, because you want to simplify the complicated big mind, it becomes a problem for you. So whether you have a problem in your life or not depends upon your own attitude, your own understanding. Because of the double or paradoxical nature of truth, there should be no problem of understanding if you have big Mahayana mind. This kind of mind will be obtained by true zazen.

N IRVANA, THE WATERFALL *"Our life and death are the same thing. When we realize this fact, we have no fear of death anymore, nor actual difficulty in our life."*

If you go to Japan and visit Eiheiji monastery, just before you enter you will see a small bridge called Hanshaku-kyo, which means "Half-Dipper Bridge." Whenever Dogen-zenji dipped water from the river, he used only half a dipperful, returning the rest to the river again, without throwing it away. That is why we call the bridge Hanshaku-kyo, "Half-Dipper Bridge." At Eiheiji when we wash our face, we fill the basin to just seventy percent of its capacity. And after we wash, we empty the water towards, rather than away from, our body. This expresses respect for the water. This kind of practice is not based on any idea of being economical. It may be difficult to understand why Dogen returned half of the water he dipped to the river. This kind of practice is beyond our thinking. When we feel the beauty of the river, when we are one with the water, we intuitively do it in Dogen's way. It is our true nature to do so. But if your true nature is covered by ideas of economy or efficiency, Dogen's way makes no sense.

I went to Yosemite National Park, and I saw some huge waterfalls. The highest one there is 1,340 feet high, and from it the water comes down like a curtain thrown from the top of the mountain. It does not seem to come down swiftly, as you might expect; it seems to come down very slowly because of the distance. And the water does not come down as one stream, but is separated into many tiny streams. From a distance it looks like a curtain. And I thought it must be a very difficult experience for each drop of water to come down from the top of such a high mountain. It takes time, you know, a long time, for the water finally to reach the bottom of the waterfall. And it seems to me that our human life may be like this. We have many difficult experiences in our life. But at the same time, I thought, the water was not originally separated, but was one whole river. Only when it is separated does it have some difficulty in falling. It is as if the water does not have any feeling when it is one whole river. Only when separated into many drops can it begin to have or to express some feeling. When we see one whole river we do not feel the living activity of the water, but when we dip a part of the water into a dipper, we experience some feeling of the water, and we also feel the value of the person who uses the water. Feeling ourselves and the water in this way, we cannot use it in just a material way. It is a living thing.

Before we were born we had no feeling; we were one with the universe. This is called "mind-only," or "essence of mind," or "big mind." After we are separated by birth from this oneness, as the water falling from the waterfall is separated by the wind and rocks, then we have feeling. You have difficulty because you have feeling. You attach to the feeling you have without knowing just how this kind of feeling is created. When you do not realize that you are one with the river, or one with the universe, you have fear. Whether it is separated into drops or not, water is water. Our life and death are the same thing. When we realize this fact we have no fear of death anymore, and we have no actual difficulty in our life.

When the water returns to its original oneness with the river, it no longer has any individual feeling to it; it resumes its own nature, and finds composure. How very glad the water must be to come back to the original river! If this is so, what feeling will we have when we die? I think we are like the water in the dipper. We will have composure then, perfect composure. It may be too perfect for us, just now, because we are so much attached to our own feeling, to our individual existence. For us, just now, we have some fear of death, but after we resume our true original nature, there is Nirvana. That is why we say, "To attain

Nirvana is to pass away." "To pass away" is not a very adequate expression. Perhaps "to pass on," or "to go on," or "to join" would be better. Will you try to find some better expression for death? When you find it, you will have quite a new interpretation of your life. It will be like my experience when I saw the water in the big waterfall. Imagine! It was 1,340 feet high!

We say, "Everything comes out of emptiness." One whole river or one whole mind is emptiness. When we reach this understanding we find the true meaning of our life. When we reach this understanding we can see the beauty of human life. Before we realize this fact, everything that we see is just delusion. Sometimes we overestimate the beauty; sometimes we underestimate or ignore the beauty because our small mind is not in accord with reality.

To talk about it this way is quite easy, but to have the actual feeling is not so easy. But by your practice of zazen you can cultivate this feeling. When you can sit with your whole body and mind, and with the oneness of your mind and body under the control of the universal mind, you can easily attain this kind of right understanding. Your everyday life will be renewed without being attached to an old erroneous interpretation of life. When you realize this fact, you will discover how meaningless your old interpretation was, and how much useless effort you had been making. You will find the true meaning of life, and even though you have difficulty falling upright from the top of the waterfall to the bottom of the mountain, you will enjoy your life.

PART THREE

Right Understanding

Our understanding of Buddhism is not just an intellectual understanding. True understanding is actual practice itself.

TRADITIONAL ZEN SPIRIT   *"If you are trying to attain enlightenment, you are creating and being driven by karma, and you are wasting your time on your black cushion."*

The most important things in our practice are our physical posture and our way of breathing. We are not so concerned about a deep understanding of Buddhism. As a philosophy, Buddhism is a very deep, wide, and firm system of thought, but Zen is not concerned about philosophical understanding. We emphasize practice. We should understand why our physical posture and breathing exercise are so important. Instead of having a deep understanding of the teaching, we need a strong confidence in our teaching, which says that originally we have Buddha nature. Our practice is based on this faith.

Before Bodhidharma went to China almost all the well-known stock words of Zen were in use. For instance, there was the term, "sudden enlightenment." "Sudden enlightenment" is not an adequate translation, but tentatively I will use the expression. Enlightenment comes all of a sudden to us. This is true enlightenment. Before Bodhidharma, people thought that after a long preparation, sudden enlightenment would come. Thus Zen practice was a kind of training to gain enlightenment. Actually, many people today are practicing zazen with this idea. But this is not the traditional understanding of Zen. The understanding passed down from Buddha to our time is that when you start zazen, there is enlightenment even without any preparation. Whether you practice zazen or not, you have Buddha nature. Because you have it, there is enlightenment in your practice. The points we emphasize are not the stage we attain, but the strong confidence we have in our original nature and the sincerity of our practice. We should practice Zen with the same sincerity as Buddha. If originally we have Buddha nature, the reason we practice zazen is that we must behave like Buddha. To transmit our way is to transmit our spirit from Buddha. So we have to harmonize our spirit, our physical posture, and our activity with the traditional way. You may attain some particular stage, of course, but the spirit of your practice should not be based on an egoistic idea.

According to the traditional Buddhist understanding, our human nature is without ego. When we have no idea of ego, we have Buddha's view of life. Our egoistic ideas are delusion, covering our Buddha nature. We are always creating and following them, and in repeating this process over and over again, our life becomes completely occupied by ego-centered ideas. This is called karmic life, or karma. The Buddhist life should not be karmic life. The purpose of our practice is to cut off the karmic spinning mind. If you are trying to attain enlightenment, that is a part of karma, you are creating and being driven by karma, and you are wasting your time on your black cushion. According to Bodhidharma's understanding, practice based on any gaining idea is just a repetition of your karma. Forgetting this point, many later Zen masters have emphasized some stage to be attained by practice.

More important than any stage which you will attain is your sincerity, your right effort. Right effort must be based on a true understanding of our traditional practice. When you understand this point you will understand how important it is to keep your posture right. When you do not understand this point, the posture and the way of breathing are just a means to attain enlightenment. If this is your attitude, it would be much better to take some drugs instead of sitting in the cross-legged position! If our practice is only a means to attain enlightenment, there is actually no way to attain it! We lose the meaning of the way to the goal. But when we believe in our way firmly, we have already attained enlightenment. When you believe in your way, enlightenment is there. But when you cannot believe in the meaning of the practice which you are doing in this moment, you cannot do anything. You are just wandering around the goal with your monkey mind. You are always looking for something without knowing what you are doing. If you want to see something, you should open your eyes. When you do not understand Bodhidharma's Zen, you are trying to look at something with your eyes closed. We do not slight the idea of attaining enlightenment, but the most important thing is this moment, not some day in the future. We have to make our effort in this moment. This is the most important thing for our practice.

Before Bodhidharma, the study of Buddha's teaching resulted in a deep and lofty philosophy of Buddhism, and people tried to attain its high ideals. This is a mistake. Bodhidharma discovered that it was a mistake to create some lofty or deep idea and then try to attain it by the practice of zazen. If that is our zazen, it is nothing different from our usual activity, or monkey mind. It looks like a very good, a very lofty and holy activity, but actually there is no difference between it and our monkey mind. That is the point that Bodhidharma emphasized.

Before Buddha attained enlightenment he made all possible efforts for us, and at last he attained a thorough understanding of the various ways. You may think Buddha attained some stage where he was free from karmic life, but it is not so. Many stories were told by Buddha about his experiences after he attained enlightenment. He was not at all different from us. When his country was at war with a powerful neighbor, he told his disciples of his own karma, of how he suffered when he saw that his country was going to be conquered by the neighboring king. If he had been someone who had attained an enlightenment in which there was no karma, there would have been no reason for him to suffer so. And even after he attained enlightenment he continued the same effort we are making. But his view of life was not shaky. His view of life was stable, and he watched everyone's life, including his own life. He watched himself, and he watched others with the same eyes that he watched stones or plants, or anything else. He had a very scientific understanding. That was his way of life after he attained enlightenment.

When we have the traditional spirit to follow the truth as it goes, and practice our way without any egoistic idea, then we will attain enlightenment in its true sense. And when we understand this point we will make our best effort in each moment. That is true understanding of Buddhism. So our understanding of Buddhism is not just an intellectual understanding. Our understanding at the same time is its own expression, *is* the practice itself. Not by reading or contemplation of philosophy, but only through practice, actual practice, can we understand what Buddhism is. Constantly, we should practice zazen, with strong confidence in our true nature, breaking the chain of karmic activity and finding our place in the world of actual practice.

T RANSIENCY *"We should find perfect existence through imperfect existence."*

The basic teaching of Buddhism is the teaching of transiency, or change. That everything changes is the basic truth for each existence. No one can deny this truth, and all the teaching of Buddhism is condensed within it. This is the teaching for all of us. Wherever we go this teaching is true. This teaching is also understood as the teaching of selflessness. Because each existence is in constant change, there is no abiding self. In fact, the self-nature of each existence is nothing but change itself, the self-nature of all existence. There is no special, separate self-nature for each existence. This is also called the teaching of Nirvana. When we realize the everlasting truth of "everything changes" and find our composure in it, we find ourselves in Nirvana.

Without accepting the fact that everything changes, we cannot find perfect composure. But unfortunately, although it is true, it is difficult for us to accept it. Because we cannot accept the truth of transiency, we suffer. So the cause of suffering is our non-acceptance of this truth. The teaching of the cause of suffering and the teaching that everything changes are thus two sides of one coin. But subjectively, transiency is the cause of our suffering. Objectively this teaching is simply the basic truth that everything changes. Dogen-zenji said, "Teaching which does not sound as if it is forcing something on you is not true teaching." The teaching itself is true, and in itself does not force anything upon us, but because of our human tendency we receive the teaching as if something was being forced on us. But whether we feel good or bad about it, this truth exists. If nothing exists, this truth does not exist. Buddhism exists because of each particular existence.

We should find perfect existence through imperfect existence. We should find perfection in imperfection. For us, complete perfection is not different from imperfection. The eternal exists because of non-eternal existence. In Buddhism it is a heretical view to expect something outside this world. We do not seek for something besides ourselves. We should find the truth in this world, through our difficulties, through our suffering. This is the basic teaching of Buddhism. Pleasure is not different from difficulty. Good is not different from bad. Bad is good; good is bad. They are two sides of one coin. So enlightenment should be in practice. That is the right understanding of practice, and the right understanding of our life. So to find pleasure in suffering is the only way to accept the truth of transiency. Without realizing how to accept this truth you cannot live in this world. Even though you try to escape from it, your effort will be in vain. If you think there is some other way to accept the eternal truth that everything changes, that is your delusion. This is the basic teaching of how to live in this world. Whatever you may feel about it, you have to accept it. You have to make this kind of effort.

So until we become strong enough to accept difficulty as pleasure, we have to continue this effort. Actually, if you become honest enough, or straightforward enough, it is not so difficult to accept this truth. You can change your way of thinking a little bit. It is difficult, but this difficulty will not always be the same. Sometimes it will be difficult, and sometimes it will not be so difficult. If you are suffering, you will have some pleasure in the teaching that everything changes. When you are in trouble, it is quite easy to accept the teaching. So why not accept it at other times? It is the same thing. Sometimes you may laugh at yourself, discovering how selfish you are. But no matter how you feel about this teaching, it is very important for you to change your way of thinking and accept the truth of transiency.

THE QUALITY OF BEING   *"When you do something, if you fix your mind on the activity with some confidence, the quality of your state of mind is the activity itself. When you are concentrated on the quality of your being, you are prepared for the activity."*

The purpose of zazen is to attain the freedom of our being, physically and mentally. According to Dogen-zenji, every existence is a flashing into the vast phenomenal world. Each existence is another expression of the quality of being itself. I often see many stars early in the morning. The stars are nothing but the light which has traveled at great speed many miles from the heavenly bodies. But for me the stars arc not speedy beings, but calm, steady, and peaceful beings. We say, "In calmness there should be activity; in activity there should be calmness." Actually, they are the same thing; to say "calmness" or to say "activity" is just to express two different interpretations of one fact. There is harmony in our activity, and where there is harmony there is calmness. This harmony is the quality of being. But the quality of being is also nothing but its speedy activity.

When we sit we feel very calm and serene, but actually we do not know what kind of activity is going on inside our being. There is complete harmony in the activity of our physical system, so we feel the calmness in it. Even if we do not feel it, the quality is there. So for us there is no need to be bothered by calmness or activity, stillness or movement. When you do something, if you fix your mind on the activity with some confidence, the quality of your state of mind is the activity itself. When you are concentrated on the quality of your being, you are prepared for the activity. Movement is nothing but the quality of our being. When we do zazen, the quality of our calm, steady, serene sitting is the quality of the immense activity of being itself.

"Everything is just a flashing into the vast phenomenal world" means the freedom of our activity and of our being. If you sit in the right manner, with the right understanding, you attain the freedom of your being, even though you are just a temporal existence. Within this moment, this temporal existence does not change, does not move, and is always independent from other existences. In the next moment another existence arises; we may change to something else. Strictly speaking, there is no connection between I myself yesterday and I myself in this moment; there is no connection whatsoever. Dogen-zenji said, "Charcoal does not become ashes." Ashes are ashes; they do not belong to charcoal. They have their own past and future. They are an independent existence because they are a flashing into the vast phenomenal world. And charcoal and red-hot fire are quite different existences. Black charcoal is also a flashing into the vast phenomenal world. Where there is black charcoal there is not red-hot charcoal. So black charcoal is independent of red-hot charcoal; ashes are independent of firewood; each existence is independent.

Today I am sitting in Los Altos. Tomorrow morning I shall be in San Francisco. There is no connection between the "I" in Los Altos and the "I" in San Francisco. They are quite different beings. Here we have the freedom of existence. And there is no quality connecting you and me; when I say "you," there is no "I"; when I say "I," there is no "you." You are independent, and I am independent; each exists in a different moment. But this does not mean we are quite different beings. We are actually one and the same being. We are the same, and yet different. It is very paradoxical, but actually it is so. Because we are independent beings, each one of us is a complete flashing into the vast phenomenal world. When I am sitting, there is no other person, but this does not mean I ignore you. I am completely one with every existence in the phenomenal world. So when I sit, you sit; everything sits with me. That is our zazen. When you sit, everything sits with you. And everything makes up the quality of your being. I am a part of you. I go into the quality of your being. So in this practice we have absolute liberation from everything else. If you understand this secret there is no difference between Zen practice and your everyday life. You can interpret everything as you wish.

A wonderful painting is the result of the feeling in your fingers. If you have the feeling of the thickness of the ink in your brush, the painting is already there before you paint. When you dip your brush into the ink you already know the result of your drawing, or else you cannot paint. So before you do something, "being" is there, the result is there. Even though you look as if you were sitting quietly, all your activity, past and present, is included; and the result of your sitting is also already there. You are not resting at all. All the activity is included within you. That is your being. So all results of your practice are included in your sitting. This is our practice, our zazen.

Dogen-zenji became interested in Buddhism as a boy as he watched the smoke from an incense stick burning by his dead mother's body, and he felt the evanescence of our life. This feeling grew within him and finally resulted in his attainment of enlightenment and the development of his deep philosophy. When he saw the smoke from the incense stick and felt the evanescence of life, he felt very lonely. But that lonely feeling became stronger and stronger, and flowered into enlightenment when he was twenty-eight years old. And at the moment of enlightenment he exclaimed, "There is no body and no mind!" When he said "no body and no mind," all his being in that moment became a flashing into the vast phenomenal world, a flashing which included everything, which covered everything, and which had immense quality in it; all the phenomenal world was included within it, an absolute independent existence. That was his enlightenment. Starting from the lonely feeling of the evanescence of life, he attained the powerful experience of the quality of his being. He said, "I have dropped off mind and body." Because you think you have body or mind, you have lonely feelings, but when you realize that everything is just a flashing into the vast universe, you become very strong, and your existence becomes very meaningful. This was Dogen's enlightenment, and this is our practice.

N ATURALNESS *"Moment after moment, everyone comes out from nothingness. This is the true joy of life."*

There is a big misunderstanding about the idea of naturalness. Most people who come to us believe in some freedom or naturalness, but their understanding is what we call *jinen ken gedo,* or heretical naturalness. *Jinen ken gedo* means that there is no need to be formal—just a kind of "let-alone policy" or sloppiness. That is naturalness for most people. But that is not the naturalness we mean. It is rather difficult to explain, but naturalness is, I think, some feeling of being independent from everything, or some activity which is based on nothingness. Something which comes out of nothingness is naturalness, like a seed or plant coming out of the ground. The seed has no idea of being some particular plant, but it has its own form and is in perfect harmony with the ground, with its surroundings. As it grows, in the course of time it expresses its nature. Nothing exists without form and color. Whatever it is, it has some form and color, and that form and color are in perfect harmony with other beings. And there is no trouble. That is what we mean by naturalness.

For a plant or stone to be natural is no problem. But for us there is some problem, indeed a big problem. To be natural is something which we must work on. When what you do just comes out from nothingness, you have quite a new feeling. For instance, when you are hungry, to take some food is naturalness. You feel natural. But when you are expecting too much, to have some food is not natural. You have no new feeling. You have no appreciation for it.

The true practice of zazen is to sit as if drinking water when you are thirsty. There you have naturalness. It is quite natural for you to take a nap when you are very sleepy. But to take a nap just because you are lazy, as if it were the privilege of a human being to take a nap, is not naturalness. You think, "My friends, all of them, are napping; why shouldn't I? When everyone else is not working, why should I work so hard? When they have a lot of money, why don't I?" This is not naturalness. Your mind is entangled with some other idea, someone else's idea, and you are not independent, not yourself, and not natural. Even if you sit in the cross-legged position, if your zazen is not natural, it is not true practice. You do not have to force yourself to drink water when you are thirsty; you are glad to drink water. If you have true joy in your zazen, that is true zazen. But even though you have to force yourself to practice zazen, if you feel something good in your practice, that is zazen. Actually it is not a matter of forcing something on you or not. Even though you have some difficulty, when you want to have it, that is naturalness.

This naturalness is very difficult to explain. But if you can just sit and experience the actuality of nothingness in your practice, there is no need to explain. If it comes out of nothingness, whatever you do is natural, and that is true activity. You have the true joy of practice, the true joy of life in it. Everyone comes out from nothingness moment after moment. Moment after moment we have true joy of life. So we say *shin ku myo u,* "from true emptiness, the wondrous being appears." *Shin* is "true"; *ku* is "emptiness"; *myo* is "wondrous"; *u* is "being": from true emptiness, wondrous being.

Without nothingness, there is no naturalness—no true being. True being comes out of nothingness, moment after moment. Nothingness is always there, and from it everything appears. But usually, forgetting all about nothingness, you behave as if you have something. What you do is based on some possessive idea or some concrete idea, and that is not natural. For instance, when you listen to a lecture, you should not have any idea of yourself. You should not have your own idea when you listen to someone. Forget what you have in your mind and just listen to what he says. To have nothing in your mind is naturalness. Then you will understand what he says. But if you have some idea to compare with what he says, you will not hear everything; your understanding will be one-sided; that is not naturalness. When you do something, you should be completely involved in it. You should devote yourself to it completely. Then you have nothing. So if there is no true emptiness in your activity, it is not natural.

Most people insist on some idea. Recently the younger generation talks about love. Love! Love! Love! Their minds are full of love! And when they study Zen, if what I say does not accord with the idea they have of love, they will not accept it. They are quite stubborn, you know. You may be amazed! Of course not all, but some have a very, very hard attitude. That is not naturalness at all. Even though they talk about love, and freedom or naturalness, they do not understand these things. And they cannot understand what Zen is in that way. If you want to study Zen, you should forget all your previous ideas and just practice zazen and see what kind of experience you have in your practice. That is naturalness.

Whatever you do, this attitude is necessary. Sometimes we say *nyu nan shin,* "soft or flexible mind." *Nyu* is "soft feeling"; *nan* is "something which is not hard"; *shin* is "mind." *Nyu nan shin* means a smooth, natural mind. When you have that mind, you have the joy of life. When you lose it, you lose everything. You have nothing. Although you think you have something, you have nothing. But when all you do comes out of nothingness, then you have everything. Do you understand? That is what we mean by naturalness.

E MPTINESS *"When you study Buddhism you should have a general house cleaning of your mind."*

If you want to understand Buddhism it is necessary for you to forget all about your preconceived ideas. To begin with, you must give up the idea of substantiality or existence. The usual view of life is firmly rooted in the idea of existence. For most people everything exists; they think whatever they see and whatever they hear exists. Of course the bird we see and hear exists. It exists, but what I mean by that may not be exactly what you mean. The Buddhist understanding of life includes both existence and non-existence. The bird both exists and does not exist at the same time. We say that a view of life based on existence alone is heretical. If you take things too seriously, as if they existed substantially or permanently, you are called a heretic. Most people may be heretics.

We say true existence comes from emptiness and goes back again into emptiness. What appears from emptiness is true existence. We have to go through the gate of emptiness. This idea of existence is very difficult to explain. Many people these days have begun to feel, at least intellectually, the emptiness of the modern world, or the self-contradiction of their culture. In the past, for instance, the Japanese people had a firm confidence in the permanent existence of their culture and their traditional way of life, but since they lost the war, they have become very skeptical. Some people think this skeptical attitude is awful, but actually it is better than the old attitude.

As long as we have some definite idea about or some hope in the future, we cannot really be serious with the moment that exists right now. You may say, "I can do it tomorrow, or next year," believing that something that exists today will exist tomorrow. Even though you are not trying so hard, you expect that some promising thing will come, as long as you follow a certain way. But there is no certain way that exists permanently. There is no way set up for us. Moment after moment we have to find our own way. Some idea of perfection, or some perfect way which is set up by someone else, is not the true way for us.

Each one of us must make his own true way, and when we do, that way will express the universal way. This is the mystery. When you understand one thing through and through, you understand everything. When you try to understand everything, you will not understand anything. The best way is to understand yourself, and then you will understand everything. So when you try hard to make your own way, you will help others, and you will be helped by others. Before you make your own way you cannot help anyone, and no one can help you. To be independent in this true sense, we have to forget everything which we have in our mind and discover something quite new and different moment after moment. This is how we live in this world.

So we say true understanding will come out of emptiness. When you study Buddhism, you should have a general house cleaning of your mind. You must take everything out of your room and clean it thoroughly. If it is necessary, you may bring everything back in again. You may want many things, so one by one you can bring them back. But if they are not necessary, there is no need to keep them.

We see the flying bird. Sometimes we see the trace of it. Actually we cannot see the trace of a flying bird, but sometimes we feel as if we could. This is also good. If it is necessary, you should bring back in the things you took from your room. But before you put something in your room, it is necessary for you to take out something. If you do not, your room will become crowded with old, useless junk.

We say, "Step by step I stop the sound of the murmuring brook." When you walk along the brook you will hear the water running. The sound is continuous, but you must be able to stop it if you want to stop it. This is freedom; this is renunciation. One after another you will have various thoughts in your mind, but if you want to stop your thinking you can. So when you are able to stop the sound of the murmuring brook, you will appreciate the feeling of your work. But as long as you have some fixed idea or are caught by some habitual way of doing things, you cannot appreciate things in their true sense.

If you seek for freedom, you cannot find it. Absolute freedom itself is necessary before you can acquire absolute freedom. That is our practice. Our way is not always to go in one direction. Sometimes we go east; sometimes we go west. To go one mile to the west means to go back one mile to the east. Usually if you go one mile to the east it is the opposite of going one mile to the west. But if it is possible to go one mile to the east, that means it is possible to go one mile to the west. This is freedom. Without this freedom you cannot be concentrated on what you do. You may think you are concentrated on something, but before you obtain this freedom, you will have some uneasiness in what you are doing. Because you are bound by some idea of going east or west, your activity is in dichotomy or duality. As long as you are caught by duality you cannot attain absolute freedom, and you cannot concentrate.

Concentration is not to try hard to watch something. In zazen if you try to look at one spot you will be tired in about five minutes. This is not concentration. Concentration means freedom. So your effort should be directed at nothing. You should be concentrated on nothing. In zazen practice we say your mind should be concentrated on your breathing, but the way to keep your mind on your breathing is to forget all about yourself and just to sit and feel your breathing. If you are concentrated on your breathing you will forget yourself, and if you forget yourself you will be concentrated on your breathing. I do not know which is first. So actually there is no need to try too hard to be concentrated on your breathing. Just do as much as you can. If you continue this practice, eventually you will experience the true existence which comes from emptiness.

R EADINESS, MINDFULNESS   *"It is the readiness of the mind that is wisdom."*

In the Prajna Paramita Sutra the most important point, of course, is the idea of emptiness. Before we understand the idea of emptiness, everything seems to exist substantially. But after we realize the emptiness of things, everything becomes real—not substantial. When we realize that everything we see is a part of emptiness, we can have no attachment to any existence; we realize that everything is just a tentative form and color. Thus we realize the true meaning of each tentative existence. When we first hear that everything is a tentative existence, most of us are disappointed; but this disappointment comes from a wrong view of man and nature. It is because our way of observing things is deeply rooted in our self-centered ideas that we are disappointed when we find everything has only a tentative existence. But when we actually realize this truth, we will have no suffering.

This sutra says, "Bodhisattva Avalokitesvara observes that everything is emptiness, thus he forsakes all suffering." It was not *after* he realized this truth that he overcame suffering—to realize this fact is itself to be relieved from suffering. So realization of the truth is salvation itself. We say, "to realize," but the realization of the truth is always near at hand. It is not after we practice zazen that we realize the truth; even before we practice zazen, realization is there. It is not after we understand the truth that we attain enlightenment. To realize the truth is to live—to exist here and now. So it is not a matter of understanding or of practice. It is an ultimate fact. In this sutra Buddha is referring to the ultimate fact that we always face moment after moment. This point is very important. This is Bodhidharma's zazen. Even before we practice it, enlightenment is there. But usually we understand the practice of zazen and enlightenment as two different things: here is practice, like a pair of glasses, and when we use the practice, like putting the glasses on, we see enlightenment. This is the wrong understanding. The glasses themselves are enlightenment, and to put them on is also enlightenment. So whatever you do, or even though you do not do anything, enlightenment is there, always. This is Bodhidharma's understanding of enlightenment.

You cannot practice true zazen, because *you* practice it; if you do not, then there is enlightenment, and there is true practice. When you do it, you create some concrete idea of "you" or "I," and you create some particular idea of practice or zazen. So here you are on the right side, and here is zazen on the left. So zazen and you become two different things. If the combination of practice and you is zazen, it is the zazen of a frog. For a frog, his sitting position is zazen. When a frog is hopping, that is not zazen. This kind of misunderstanding will vanish if you really understand emptiness means everything is always here. One whole being is not an accumulation of everything. It is impossible to divide one whole existence into parts. It is always here and always working. This is enlightenment. So there actually is no particular practice. In the sutra it says, "There are no eyes, no ears, no nose, no tongue, no body or mind. . . ." This "no mind" is Zen mind, which includes everything.

The important thing in our understanding is to have a smooth, free-thinking way of observation. We have to think and to observe things without stagnation. We should accept things as they are without difficulty. Our mind should be soft and open enough to understand things as they are. When our thinking is soft, it is called imperturbable thinking. This kind of thinking is always stable. It is called mindfulness. Thinking which is divided in many ways is not true thinking. Concentration should be present in our thinking. This is mindfulness. Whether you have an object or not, your mind should be stable and your mind should not be divided. This is zazen.

It is not necessary to make an effort to think in a particular way. Your thinking should not be one-sided. We just think with our whole mind, and see things as they are without any effort. Just to see, and to be ready to see things with our whole mind, is zazen practice. If we are prepared for thinking, there is no need to make an effort to think. This is called mindfulness. Mindfulness is, at the same time, wisdom. By wisdom we do not mean some particular faculty or philosophy. It is the readiness of the mind that is wisdom. So wisdom could be various philosophies and teachings, and various kinds of research and studies. But we should not become attached to some particular wisdom, such as that which was taught by Buddha. Wisdom is not something to learn. Wisdom is something which will come out of your mindfulness. So the point is to be ready for observing things, and to be ready for thinking. This is called emptiness of your mind. Emptiness is nothing but the practice of zazen.

B ELIEVING IN NOTHING   *"In our everyday life our thinking is ninety-nine percent self-centered. 'Why do I have suffering? Why do I have trouble?'"*

I discovered that it is necessary, absolutely necessary, to believe in nothing. That is, we have to believe in something which has no form and no color—something which exists before all forms and colors appear. This is a very important point. No matter what god or doctrine you believe in, if you become attached to it, your belief will be based more or less on a self-centered idea. You strive for a perfect faith in order to save yourself. But it will take time to attain such a perfect faith. You will be involved in an idealistic practice. In constantly seeking to actualize your ideal, you will have no time for composure. But if you are always prepared for accepting everything we see as something appearing from nothing, knowing that there is some reason why a phenomenal existence of such and such form and color appears, then at that moment you will have perfect composure.

When you have a headache, there is some reason why

you have a headache. If you know why you have a headache, you will feel better. But if you do not know why, you may say, "Oh, I have a terrible headache! Maybe it is because of my bad practice. If my meditation or Zen practice were better I wouldn't have this kind of trouble!" If you understand conditions in this way you will not have perfect faith in yourself, or in your practice, until you attain perfection. You will be so busy trying that I am afraid you will have no time to attain perfect practice, so you may have to keep your headache all the time! This is a rather silly kind of practice. This kind of practice will not work. But if you believe in something which exists before you had the headache, and if you know the reason why you have the headache, then you will feel better, naturally. To have a headache will be all right, because you are healthy enough to have a headache. If you have a stomachache, your stomach is healthy enough to have pain. But if your stomach becomes accustomed to its poor condition, you will have no pain. That is awful! You will be coming to the end of your life from your stomach trouble.

So it is absolutely necessary for everyone to believe in nothing. But I do not mean voidness. There is something, but that something is something which is always prepared for taking some particular form, and it has some rules, or theory, or truth in its activity. This is called Buddha nature, or Buddha himself. When this existence is personified we call it Buddha; when we understand it as the ultimate truth we call it Dharma; and when we accept the truth and act as a part of the Buddha, or according to the theory, we call ourselves Sangha. But even though there are three Buddha forms, it is one existence which has no form or color, and it is always ready to take form and color. This is not just theory. This is not just the teaching of Buddhism. This is the absolutely necessary understanding of our life. Without this understanding our religion will not help us. We will be bound by our religion, and we will have more trouble because of it. If you become the victim of Buddhism, I may be very happy, but you will not be so happy. So this kind of understanding is very, very important.

While you are practicing zazen, you may hear the rain dropping from the roof in the dark. Later, the wonderful mist will be coming through the big trees, and still later when people start to work, they will see the beautiful mountains. But some people will be annoyed if they hear the rain when they are lying in their beds in the morning, because they do not know that later they will see the beautiful sun rising from the east. If our mind is concentrated on ourselves we will have this kind of worry. But if we accept ourselves as the embodiment of the truth, or Buddha nature, we will have no worry. We will think, "Now it is raining, but we don't know what will happen in the next moment. By the time we go out it may be a beautiful day, or a stormy day. Since we don't know, let's appreciate the sound of the rain now." This kind of attitude is the right attitude. If you understand yourself as a temporal embodiment of the truth, you will have no difficulty whatsoever. You will appreciate your surroundings, and you will appreciate yourself as a wonderful part of Buddha's great activity, even in the midst of difficulties. This is our way of life.

Using the Buddhist terminology, we should begin with enlightenment and proceed to practice, and then to thinking. Usually thinking is rather self-centered. In our everyday life our thinking is ninety-nine percent self-centered: "Why do I have suffering? Why do I have trouble?" This kind of thinking is ninety-nine percent of our thinking. For example, when we start to study science or read a difficult sutra, we very soon become sleepy or drowsy. But we are always wide awake and very much interested in our self-centered thinking! But if enlightenment comes first, before thinking, before practice, your thinking and your practice will not be self-centered. By enlightenment I mean believing in nothing, believing in something which has no form or no color, which is ready to take form or color. This enlightenment is the immutable truth. It is on this original truth that our activity, our thinking, and our practice should be based.

A TTACHMENT, NONATTACHMENT *"That we are attached to some beauty is also Buddha's activity."*

Dogen-zenji said, "Even though it is midnight, dawn is here; even though dawn comes, it is nighttime." This kind of statement conveys the understanding transmitted from Buddha to the Patriarchs, and from the Patriarchs to Dogen, and to us. Nighttime and daytime are not different. The same thing is sometimes called nighttime, sometimes called daytime. They are one thing.

Zazen practice and everyday activity are one thing. We call zazen everyday life, and everyday life zazen. But usually we think, "Now zazen is over, and we will go about our everyday activity." But this is not the right understanding. They are the same thing. We have nowhere to escape. So in activity there should be calmness, and in calmness there should be activity. Calmness and activity are not different.

Each existence depends on something else. Strictly speaking, there are no separate individual existences. There are just many names for one existence. Sometimes people put stress on oneness, but this is not our understanding. We do not emphasize any point in particular, even oneness. Oneness is valuable, but variety is also wonderful. Ignoring variety, people emphasize the one absolute existence, but this is a one-sided understanding. In this understanding there is a gap between variety and oneness. But oneness and variety are the same thing, so oneness should be appreciated in each existence. That is why we emphasize everyday life rather than some particular state of mind. We should find the reality in each moment, and in each phenomenon. This is a very important point.

Dogen-zenji said, "Although everything has Buddha nature, we love flowers, and we do not care for weeds." This is true of human nature. But that we are attached to some beauty is itself Buddha's activity. That we do not care for weeds is also Buddha's activity. We should know that. If you know that, it is all right to attach to something. If it is Buddha's attachment, that is non-attachment. So in love there should be hate, or nonattachment. And in hate there should be love, or acceptance. Love and hate are one thing. We should not attach to love alone. We should accept hate. We should accept weeds, despite how we feel about them. If you do not care for them, do not love them; if you love them, then love them.

Usually you criticize yourself for being unfair to your surroundings; you criticize your unaccepting attitude. But there is a very subtle difference between the usual way of accepting and our way of accepting things, although they may seem exactly the same. We have been taught that there is no gap between nighttime and daytime, no gap between you and I. This means oneness. But we do not emphasize even oneness. If it is one, there is no need to emphasize one.

Dogen said, "To learn something is to know yourself; to study Buddhism is to study yourself." To learn something is not to acquire something which you did not know before. You know something before you learn it. There is no gap between the "I" before you know something and the "I" after you know something. There is no gap between the ignorant and the wise. A foolish person is a wise person; a wise person is a foolish person. But usually we think, "*He* is foolish and *I* am wise," or "I *was* foolish, but now I am wise." How can we be wise if we are foolish? But the understanding transmitted from Buddha to us is that there is no difference whatsoever between the foolish man and the wise man. It is so. But if I say this people may think that I am emphasizing oneness. This is not so. We do not emphasize anything. All we want to do is to know things just as they are. If we know things as they are, there is nothing to point at; there is no way to grasp anything; there is no thing to grasp. We cannot put emphasis on any point. Nevertheless, as Dogen said, "A flower falls, even though we love it; and a weed grows, even though we do not love it." Even though it is so, this is our life.

In this way our life should be understood. Then there is no problem. Because we put emphasis on some particular point, we always have trouble. We should accept things just as they are. This is how we understand everything, and how we live in this world. This kind of experience is something beyond our thinking. In the thinking realm there is a difference between oneness and variety; but in actual experience, variety and unity are the same. Because you create some idea of unity or variety, you are caught by the idea. And you have to continue the endless thinking, although actually there is no need to think.

Emotionally we have many problems, but these problems are not actual problems; they are something created; they are problems pointed out by our self-centered ideas or views. Because we point out something, there are problems. But actually it is not possible to point out anything in particular. Happiness is sorrow; sorrow is happiness. There is happiness in difficulty; difficulty in happiness. Even though the ways we feel are different, they are not really different; in essence they are the same. This is the true understanding transmitted from Buddha to us.

CALMNESS   *"For Zen students a weed is a treasure."*

A Zen poem says, "After the wind stops I see a flower falling. Because of the singing bird I find the mountain calmness." Before something happens in the realm of calmness, we do not feel the calmness; only when something happens within it do we find the calmness. There is a Japanese saying, "For the moon there is the cloud. For the flower there is the wind." When we see a part of the moon covered by a cloud, or a tree, or a weed, we feel how round the moon is. But when we see the clear moon without anything covering it, we do not feel that roundness the same way we do when we see it through something else.

When you are doing zazen, you are within the complete

calmness of your mind; you do not feel anything. You just sit. But the calmness of your sitting will encourage you in your everyday life. So actually you will find the value of Zen in your everyday life, rather than while you sit. But this does not mean you should neglect zazen. Even though you do not feel anything when you sit, if you do not have this zazen experience, you cannot find anything; you just find weeds, or trees, or clouds in your daily life; you do not see the moon. That is why you are always complaining about something. But for Zen students a weed, which for most people is worthless, is a treasure. With this attitude, whatever you do, life becomes an art.

When you practice zazen you should not try to attain anything. You should just sit in the complete calmness of your mind and not rely on anything. Just keep your body straight without leaning over or against something. To keep your body straight means not to rely on anything. In this way, physically and mentally, you will obtain complete calmness. But to rely on something or to try to do something in zazen is dualistic and not complete calmness.

In our everyday life we are usually trying to do something, trying to change something into something else, or trying to attain something. Just this trying is already in itself an expression of our true nature. The meaning lies in the effort itself. We should find out the meaning of our effort before we attain something. So Dogen said, "We should attain enlightenment before we attain enlightenment." It is not after attaining enlightenment that we find its true meaning. The trying to do something in itself is enlightenment. When we are in difficulty or distress, there we have enlightenment. When we are in defilement, there we should have composure. Usually we find it very difficult to live in the evanescence of life, but it is only within the evanescence of life that we can find the joy of eternal life.

By continuing your practice with this sort of understanding, you can improve yourself. But if you try to attain something without this understanding you cannot work on it properly. You lose yourself in the struggle for your goal; you achieve nothing; you just continue to suffer in your difficulties. But with right understanding you can make some progress. Then whatever you do, even though not perfect, will be based on your inmost nature, and little by little something will be achieved.

Which is more important: to attain enlightenment, or to attain enlightenment before you attain enlightenment; to make a million dollars, or to enjoy your life in your effort, little by little, even though it is impossible to make that million; to be successful, or to find some meaning in your effort to be successful? If you do not know the answer, you will not even be able to practice zazen; if you do know, you will have found the true treasure of life.

EXPERIENCE, NOT PHILOSOPHY   *"There is something blasphemous in talking about how Buddhism is perfect as a philosophy or teaching without knowing what it actually is."*

Although there are many people in this country who are interested in Buddhism, few of them are interested in its pure form. Most of them are interested in studying the teaching or the philosophy of Buddhism. Comparing it to other religions, they appreciate how satisfying Buddhism is intellectually. But whether Buddhism is philosophically deep or good or perfect is not the point. To keep our practice in its pure form is our purpose. Sometimes I feel there is something blasphemous in talking about how Buddhism is perfect as a philosophy or teaching without knowing what it actually is.

To practice zazen with a group is the most important thing for Buddhism—and for us—because this practice is the original way of life. Without knowing the origin of things we cannot appreciate the result of our life's effort. Our effort must have some meaning. To find the meaning of our effort is to find the original source of our effort. We should not be concerned about the result of our effort before we know its origin. If the origin is not clear and pure, our effort will not be pure, and its result will not satisfy us. When we resume our original nature and incessantly make our effort from this base, we will appreciate the result of our effort moment after moment, day after day, year after year. This is how we should appreciate our life. Those who are attached only to the result of their effort will not have any chance to appreciate it, because the result will never come. But if moment by moment your effort arises from its pure origin, all you do will be good, and you will be satisfied with whatever you do.

Zazen practice is the practice in which we resume our pure way of life, beyond any gaining idea, and beyond fame and profit. By practice we just keep our original nature as it is. There is no need to intellectualize about what our pure original nature is, because it is beyond our intellectual understanding. And there is no need to appreciate it, because it is beyond our appreciation. So just to sit, without any idea of gain, and with the purest intention, to remain as quiet as our original nature—this is our practice.

In the zendo there is nothing fancy. We just come and sit. After communicating with each other we go home and resume our own everyday activity as a continuity of our pure practice, enjoying our true way of life. Yet this is very unusual. Wherever I go people ask me, "What is Buddhism?" with their notebooks ready to write down my answer. You can imagine how I feel! But here we just practice zazen. That is all we do, and we are happy in this practice. For us there is no need to understand what Zen is. We are practicing zazen. So for us there is no need to know what Zen is intellectually. This is, I think, very unusual for American society.

In America there are many patterns of life and many religions, so it may seem quite natural to talk about the differences between the various religions and compare one with the other. But for us there is no need to compare Buddhism to Christianity. Buddhism is Buddhism, and Buddhism is our practice. We do not even know what we are doing when we just practice with a pure mind. So we cannot compare our way to some other religion. Some people may say that Zen Buddhism is not religion. Maybe that is so, or maybe Zen Buddhism is religion before religion. So it might not be religion in the usual sense. But it is wonderful, and even though we do not study what it is intellectually, even though we do not have any cathedral or fancy ornaments, it is possible to appreciate our original nature. This is, I think, quite unusual.

ORIGINAL BUDDHISM   *"Actually, we are not the Soto school at all. We are just Buddhists. We are not even Zen Buddhists. If we understand this point, we are truly Buddhists."*

Walking, standing, sitting, and lying down are the four activities or ways of behavior in Buddhism. Zazen is not one of the four ways of behavior, and according to Dogen-zenji, the Soto school is not one of the many schools of Buddhism. The Chinese Soto school may be one of the many schools of Buddhism, but according to Dogen, his way was not one of the many schools. If this is so, you may ask why we put emphasis on the sitting posture or why we put emphasis on having a teacher. The reason is because zazen is not just one of the four ways of behavior. Zazen is a practice which contains innumerable activities; zazen started even before Buddha, and will continue forever. So this sitting posture cannot be compared to the other four activities.

Usually people put emphasis on some particular position or on some particular understanding of Buddhism, and they think, "This is Buddhism!" But we cannot compare our way with the practices people normally understand. Our teaching cannot be compared to other teachings of Buddhism. This is why we should have a teacher who does not attach to any particular understanding of Buddhism. The original teaching of Buddha includes all the various schools. As Buddhists our traditional effort should be like Buddha's: we should not attach to any particular school or doctrine. But usually, if we have no teacher, and if we take pride in our own understanding, we will lose the original characteristic of Buddha's teaching, which includes all the various teachings.

Because Buddha was the founder of the teaching, people tentatively called his teaching "Buddhism," but actually Buddhism is not some particular teaching. Buddhism is just Truth, which includes various truths in it. Zazen practice is the practice which includes the various activities of life. So actually, we do not emphasize the sitting posture alone. How to sit is how to act. We study how to act by sitting, and this is the most basic activity for us. That is why we practice zazen in this way. Even though we practice zazen, we should not call ourselves the Zen school. We just practice zazen, taking our example from Buddha; that is why we practice. Buddha taught us how to act through our practice; that is why we sit.

To do something, to live in each moment, means to be the temporal activity of Buddha. To sit in this way is to be Buddha himself, to be as the historical Buddha was. The same thing applies to everything we do. Everything is Buddha's activity. So whatever you do, or even if you keep from doing something, Buddha is in that activity. Because people have no such understanding of Buddha, they think what they do is the most important thing, without knowing who it is that is actually doing it. People think they are doing various things, but actually Buddha is doing everything. Each one of us has his own name, but those names are the many names of one Buddha. Each one of us has many activities, but those activities are all Buddha's activities. Without knowing this, people put emphasis on some activity. When they put emphasis on zazen, it is not true zazen. It looks as if they were sitting in the same way as Buddha, but there is a big difference in their understanding of our practice. They understand this sitting posture as just one of the four basic postures of man, and they think: "I now take this posture." But zazen is all the postures, and each posture is Buddha's posture. This understanding is the right understanding of the zazen posture. If you practice in this way, it is Buddhism. This is a very, very important point.

So Dogen did not call himself a Soto teacher or a Soto disciple. He said, "Other people may call us the Soto school, but there is no reason for us to call ourselves Soto. You should not even use the name of Soto." No school should consider itself a separate school. It should just be one tentative form of Buddhism. But as long as the various schools do not accept this kind of understanding, as long as they continue calling themselves by their particular names, we must accept the tentative name of Soto. But I want to make this point clear. Actually we are not the Soto school at all. We are just Buddhists. We are not even Zen Buddhists; we are just Buddhists. If we understand this point we are truly Buddhists.

Buddha's teaching is everywhere. Today it is raining. This is Buddha's teaching. People think their own way or their own religious understanding is Buddha's way, without knowing what they are hearing, or what they are doing, or where they are. Religion is not any particular teaching. Religion is everywhere. We have to understand our teaching in this way. We should forget all about some particular teaching; we should not ask which is good or bad. There should not be any particular teaching. Teaching is in each moment, in every existence. That is the true teaching.

B EYOND CONSCIOUSNESS *"To realize pure mind in your delusion is practice. If you try to expel the delusion it will only persist the more. Just say, 'Oh, this is just delusion,' and do not be bothered by it."*

We should establish our practice where there is no practice or enlightenment. As long as we practice zazen in the area where there is practice and enlightenment, there is no chance to make perfect peace for ourselves. In other words, we must firmly believe in our true nature. Our true nature is beyond our conscious experience. It is only in our conscious experience that we find practice and enlightenment or good and bad. But whether or not we have experience of our true nature, what exists there, beyond consciousness, actually exists, and it is there that we have to establish the foundation of our practice.

Even to have a good thing in your mind is not so good. Buddha sometimes said, "You should be like this. You ought not to be like that." But to have what he says in your mind is not so good. It is a kind of burden for you, and you may not actually feel so good. In fact to harbor some ill will may even be better than to have some idea in your mind of what is good or of what you ought to do. To have some mischievous idea in your mind is sometimes very agreeable. That is true. Actually, good and bad is not the point. Whether or not you make yourself peaceful is the point, and whether or not you stick to it.

When you have something in your consciousness you do not have perfect composure. The best way towards perfect composure is to forget everything. Then your mind is calm, and it is wide and clear enough to see and feel things

as they are without any effort. The best way to find perfect composure is not to retain any idea of things, whatever
they may be—to forget all about them and not to leave
any trace or shadow of thinking. But if you try to stop your
mind or try to go beyond your conscious activity, that will
only be another burden for you. "I have to stop my mind in
my practice, but I cannot. My practice is not so good." This
kind of idea is also the wrong way of practice. Do not try
to stop your mind, but leave everything as it is. Then things
will not stay in your mind so long. Things will come as they
come and go as they go. Then eventually your clear, empty
mind will last fairly long.

So to have a firm conviction in the original emptiness
of your mind is the most important thing in your practice.
In Buddhist scriptures we sometimes use vast analogies in
an attempt to describe empty mind. Sometimes we use an
astronomically great number, so great it is beyond counting. This means to give up calculating. If it is so great that
you cannot count it, then you will lose your interest and
eventually give up. This kind of description may also give
rise to a kind of interest in the innumerable number, which
will help you to stop the thinking of your small mind.

But it is when you sit in zazen that you will have the
most pure, genuine experience of the empty state of mind.
Actually, emptiness of mind is not even a state of mind, but
the original essence of mind which Buddha and the Sixth
Patriarch experienced. "Essence of mind," "original mind,"
"original face," "Buddha nature," "emptiness"—all these
words mean the absolute calmness of our mind.

You know how to rest physically. You do not know how
to rest mentally. Even though you lie in your bed your mind
is still busy; even if you sleep your mind is busy dreaming.

Your mind is always in intense activity. This is not so good. We should know how to give up our thinking mind, our busy mind. In order to go beyond our thinking faculty, it is necessary to have a firm conviction in the emptiness of your mind. Believing firmly in the perfect rest of our mind, we should resume our pure original state.

Dogen-zenji said, "You should establish your practice in your delusion." Even though you think you are in delusion, your pure mind is there. To realize pure mind in your delusion is practice. If you have pure mind, essential mind in your delusion, the delusion will vanish. It cannot stay when you say, "This is delusion!" It will be very much ashamed. It will run away. So you should establish your practice in your delusion. To have delusion is practice. This is to attain enlightenment before you realize it. Even though you do not realize it, you have it. So when you say, "This is delusion," that is actually enlightenment itself. If you try to expel the delusion it will only persist the more, and your mind will become busier and busier trying to cope with it. That is not so good. Just say, "Oh, this is just delusion," and do not be bothered by it. When you just observe the delusion, you have your true mind, your calm, peaceful mind. When you start to cope with it you will be involved in delusion.

So whether or not you attain enlightenment, just to sit in zazen is enough. When you try to attain enlightenment, then you have a big burden on your mind. Your mind will not be clear enough to see things as they are. If you truly see things as they are, then you will see things as they should be. On the one hand, we should attain enlightenment—that is how things should be. But on the other hand, as long as we are physical beings, in reality it is pretty hard to attain enlightenment—that is how things actually are in this moment. But if we start to sit, both sides of our nature will be brought up, and we will see things both as they are and as they should be. Because we are not good right now, we want to be better, but when we attain the transcendental mind, we go beyond things as they are and as they should be. In the emptiness of our original mind they are one, and there we find our perfect composure.

Usually religion develops itself in the realm of consciousness, seeking to perfect its organization, building beautiful buildings, creating music, evolving a philosophy, and so forth. These are religious activities in the conscious world. But Buddhism emphasizes the world of unconsciousness. The best way to develop Buddhism is to sit in zazen—just to sit, with a firm conviction in our true nature. This way is much better than to read books or study the philosophy of Buddhism. Of course it is necessary to study the philosophy—it will strengthen your conviction. Buddhist philosophy is so universal and logical that it is not just the philosophy of Buddhism, but of life itself. The purpose of Buddhist teaching is to point to life itself existing beyond consciousness in our pure original mind. All Buddhist practices were built up to protect this true teaching, not to propagate Buddhism in some wonderful mystic way. So when we discuss religion, it should be in the most common and universal way. We should not try to propagate our way by wonderful philosophical thought. In some ways Buddhism is rather polemical, with some feeling of controversy in it, because the Buddhist must protect his way from mystic or magical interpretations of religion. But philosophical discussion will not be the best way to understand Buddhism. If you want to be a sincere

Buddhist, the best way is to sit. We are very fortunate to have a place to sit in this way. I want you to have a firm, wide, imperturbable conviction in your zazen of just sitting. Just to sit, that is enough.

B UDDHA'S ENLIGHTENMENT   *"If you take pride in your attainment or become discouraged because of your idealistic effort, your practice will confine you by a thick wall."*

I am very glad to be here on the day Buddha attained enlightenment under the Bo tree. When he attained enlightenment under the Bo tree, he said, "It is wonderful to see Buddha nature in everything and in each individual!" What he meant was that when we practice zazen we have Buddha nature, and each of us is Buddha himself. By practice he did not mean just to sit under the Bo tree, or to sit in the cross-legged posture. It is true that this posture is the basic one or original way for us, but actually what Buddha meant was that mountains, trees, flowing water, flowers, and plants—everything as it is—is the way Buddha is. It means everything is taking Buddha's activity, each thing in its own way.

But the way each thing exists is not to be understood by itself in its own realm of consciousness. What we see or what we hear is just a part, or a limited idea, of what we actually are. But when we just are—each just existing in his own way—we are expressing Buddha himself. In other words, when we practice something such as zazen, then there is Buddha's way or Buddha nature. When we ask what Buddha nature is, it vanishes; but when we just practice zazen, we have full understanding of it. The only way to understand Buddha nature is just to practice zazen, just to be here as we are. So what Buddha meant by Buddha nature was to be there as he was, beyond the realm of consciousness.

Buddha nature is our original nature; we have it before we practice zazen and before we acknowledge it in terms of consciousness. So in this sense, whatever we do is Buddha's activity. If you want to understand it, you cannot understand it. When you give up trying to understand it, true understanding is always there. Usually after zazen I give a talk, but the reason people come is not just to listen to my talk, but to practice zazen. We should never forget this point. The reason I talk is to encourage you to practice zazen in Buddha's way. So we say that although you have Buddha nature, if you are under the idea of doing or not doing zazen, or if you cannot admit that you are Buddha, then you understand neither Buddha nature nor zazen. But when you practice zazen in the same way as Buddha did, you will understand what our way is. We do not talk so much, but through our activity we communicate with each other, intentionally or unintentionally. We should always be alert enough to communicate with or without words. If this point is lost, we will lose the most important point of Buddhism.

Wherever we go, we should not lose this way of life. That is called "being Buddha," or "being the boss." Wherever you go you should be the master of your surroundings. This means you should not lose your way. So this is called Buddha, because if you exist in this way always, you are Buddha himself. Without trying to be Buddha you are

Buddha. This is how we attain enlightenment. To attain enlightenment is to be always with Buddha. By repeating the same thing over and over, we will acquire this kind of understanding. But if you lose this point and take pride in your attainment or become discouraged because of your idealistic effort, your practice will confine you by a thick wall. We should not confine ourselves by a self-built wall. So when zazen time comes, just to get up, to go and sit with your teacher, and to talk to him and listen to him, and then go home again—all these procedures are our practice. In this way, without any idea of attainment, you are always Buddha. This is true practice of zazen. Then you may understand the true meaning of Buddha's first statement, "See Buddha nature in various beings, and in every one of us."

EPILOGUE

ZEN MIND   *"Before the rain stops we can hear a bird. Even under the heavy snow we see snowdrops and some new growth."*

Here in America we cannot define Zen Buddhists the same way we do in Japan. American students are not priests and yet not completely laymen. I understand it this way: that you are not priests is an easy matter, but that you are not exactly laymen is more difficult. I think you are special people and want some special practice that is not exactly priests' practice and not exactly laymen's practice. You are on your way to discovering some appropriate way of life. I think that is our Zen community, our group.

But we must also know what our undivided original way is and what Dogen's practice is. Dogen-zenji said that some may attain enlightenment and some may not. This is a point I am very much interested in. Although we all have the same fundamental practice which we carry out in the same way, some may attain enlightenment and some may not. It means that even if we have no experience of enlightenment, if we sit in the proper way with the right attitude and understanding of practice, then that is Zen. The main point is to practice seriously, and the important attitude is to understand and have confidence in big mind.

We say "big mind," or "small mind," or "Buddha mind," or "Zen mind," and these words mean something, you know, but something we cannot and should not try to understand in terms of experience. We talk about enlightenment experience, but it is not some experience we will have in terms of good or bad, time or space, past or future. It is experience or consciousness beyond those distinctions or feelings. So we should not ask, "What is enlightenment experience?" That kind of question means you do not know what Zen experience is. Enlightenment cannot be asked for in your ordinary way of thinking. When you are not involved in this way of thinking, you have some chance of understanding what Zen experience is.

The big mind in which we must have confidence is not something which you can experience objectively. It is something which is always with you, always on your side. Your eyes are on your side, for you cannot see your eyes, and your eyes cannot see themselves. Eyes only see things outside, objective things. If you reflect on yourself, that self is not your true self any more. You cannot project yourself as some objective thing to think about. The mind which is always on your side is not just your mind, it is universal mind, always the same, not different from another's mind. It is Zen mind. It is big, big mind. This mind is whatever you see. Your true mind is always with whatever you see. Although you do not know your own mind, it is there—at the very moment you see something, it is there. This is very interesting. Your mind is always with the things you observe. So you see, this mind is at the same time everything.

True mind is watching mind. You cannot say, "This is my self, my small mind, or my limited mind, and that is big mind." That is limiting yourself, restricting your true mind, objectifying your mind. Bodhidharma said, "In order to see a fish you must watch the water." Actually when you see water you see the true fish. Before you see Buddha nature you watch your mind. When you see the water there is true nature. True nature is watching water. When you say, "My zazen is very poor," here you have true nature, but foolishly you do not realize it. You ignore it on purpose. There is immense importance in the "I" with which you watch your mind. That I is not the "big I"; it is the "I" which is incessantly active, always swimming, always flying through the vast air with wings. By wings I mean thought and activity. The vast sky is home, my home. There is no bird or air. When the fish swims, water and fish are the fish. There is nothing but fish. Do you understand? You cannot find Buddha nature by vivisection. Reality cannot be caught by thinking or feeling mind. Moment after moment to watch your breathing, to watch your posture, is true nature. There is no secret beyond this point.

We Buddhists do not have any idea of material only, or mind only, or the products of our mind, or mind as an attribute of being. What we are always talking about is that mind and body, mind and material are always one. But if you listen carelessly it sounds as if we are talking about some attribute of being, or about "material" or "spiritual." That will be a version of it, maybe. But actually we are pointing out mind which is always on this side, which is true mind. Enlightenment experience is to figure out, to understand, to realize this mind which is always with us and which we cannot see. Do you understand? If you try to attain enlightenment as if you see a bright star in the sky, it will be beautiful and you may think, "Ah, this is enlightenment," but that is not enlightenment. That understanding is literally heresy. Even though you do not know it, in that understanding you have the idea of material only. Dozens of your enlightenment experiences are like that—some material only, some object of your mind, as if through good practice you found that bright star. That is the idea of self and object. It is not the way to seek for enlightenment.

The Zen school is based on our actual nature, on our true mind as expressed and realized in practice. Zen does not depend on a particular teaching nor does it substitute teaching for practice. We practice zazen to express our true nature, not to attain enlightenment. Bodhidharma's Buddhism is to *be* practice, to *be* enlightenment. At first this may be a kind of belief, but later it is something the student feels or already has. Physical practice and rules are not so easy to understand, maybe especially for Americans. You have an idea of freedom which concentrates on physical freedom, on freedom of activity. This idea causes you some mental suffering and loss of freedom. You think you want to limit your thinking, you think some of your thinking is unnecessary or painful or entangling; but you do not think you want to limit your physical activity. For this reason Hyakujo established the rules and way of Zen life in China. He was interested in expressing and transmitting the freedom of true mind. Zen mind is transmitted in our Zen way of life based on Hyakujo's rules.

I think we naturally need some way of life as a group and as Zen students in America, and as Hyakujo established our way of monastic life in China, I think we must establish an American way of Zen life. I am not saying this jokingly, I am pretty serious. But I do not want to be too serious. If we become too serious we will lose our way. If we are playing games we will lose our way. Little by little with patience and endurance we must find the way for ourselves, find out how to live with ourselves and with each other. In this way we will find out our precepts. If we practice hard, concentrate on zazen, and organize our life so that we can sit well, we will find out what we are doing. But you have to be careful in the rules and way you establish. If it is too strict you will fail, if it is too loose, the rules will not work. Our way should be strict enough to have authority, an authority everyone should obey. The rules should be possible to observe. This is how Zen tradition was built up, decided little by little, created by us in our practice. We cannot force anything. But once the rules have been decided, we should obey them completely until they are changed. It is not a matter of good or bad, convenient or inconvenient. You just do it without question. That way your mind is free. The important thing is to obey your rules without discrimination. This way you will know the pure Zen mind. To have our own way of life means to encourage people to have a more spiritual and adequate way of life as human beings. And I think one day you will have your own practice in America.

The only way to study pure mind is through practice. Our inmost nature wants some medium, some way to express and realize itself. We answer this inmost request through our rules, and Patriarch after Patriarch shows us his true mind. In this way we will have an accurate, deep understanding of practice. We must have more experience of our practice. At least we must have *some* enlightenment experience. You must put confidence in the big mind which is always with you. You should be able to appreciate things as an expression of big mind. This is more than faith. This is ultimate truth which you cannot reject. Whether it is difficult or easy to practice, difficult or easy to understand, you can only practice it. Priest or layman is not the point. To find yourself as someone who is doing something is the point—to resume your actual being through practice, to resume the you which is always with everything, with Buddha, which is fully supported by everything. Right now! You may say it is impossible. But it is possible! Even in one moment you can do it! It is possible this moment! It is this moment! That you can do it in this moment means you can always do it. So if you have this confidence, this is your enlightenment experience. If you have this strong confidence in your big mind, you are already a Buddhist in the true sense, even though you do not attain enlightenment.

That is why Dogen-zenji said, "Do not expect that all who practice zazen will attain enlightenment about this mind which is always with us." He meant if you think that big mind is somewhere outside yourself, outside of your practice, then that is a mistake. Big mind is always with us. That is why I repeat the same thing over and over when I think you do not understand. Zen is not just for the man who can fold his legs or who has great spiritual ability. Everyone has Buddha nature. We each must find some way to realize our true nature. The purpose of practice is to have direct experience of the Buddha nature which everyone has. Whatever you do should be the direct experience of Buddha nature. Buddha nature means to be aware of Buddha nature. Your effort should extend to saving all sentient beings. If my words are not good enough, I'll hit you! Then you will understand what I mean. And if you do not understand me just now, some day you will. Some day someone will understand. I will wait for the island I was told is moving slowly up the coast from Los Angeles to Seattle.

I feel Americans, especially young Americans, have a great opportunity to find out the true way of life for human beings. You are quite free from material things and you begin Zen practice with a very pure mind, a beginner's mind. You can understand Buddha's teaching exactly as he meant it. But we must not be attached to America, or Buddhism, or even to our practice. We must have beginner's mind, free from possessing anything, a mind that knows everything is in flowing change. Nothing exists but momentarily in its present form and color. One thing flows into another and cannot be grasped. Before the rain stops we hear a bird. Even under the heavy snow we see snowdrops and some new growth. In the East I saw rhubarb already. In Japan in the spring we eat cucumbers.

AFTERWORD

Zen Mind, Beginner's Mind at Forty

When Shunryu Suzuki first saw a published copy of *Zen Mind, Beginner's Mind,* he looked it over for a minute and commented, "Good book. I didn't write it, but it looks like a good book."

That was forty years ago, the summer of 1970. He and a few students were in the foyer of the San Francisco Zen Center's City Center standing around some boxes of the newly published hardcover.

More than forty years before that, in the early 1920s, as a young Zen monk strolling through the shops and stands in the bustling trade city of Yokohama, Suzuki had lamented the poor quality of Japanese furniture, toys, and other items bound for export. He wondered why they didn't send abroad the best of their crafts and arts. Maybe someday, he thought, if he studied and applied himself sincerely, he could bring to the West what to him was truly the best his homeland had to offer: the way of his Zen mentors. He never completely let go of that idea, and eventually the knots of duty loosened, an opportunity arose, and he flew to San Francisco carrying a painting and a hidden plant.

Most of Suzuki's students didn't get too excited when *Zen Mind, Beginner's Mind* came out. We had him and he told us to forget what he said in lectures and instead to put our effort wholeheartedly into zazen and mindfulness.

People did study, but his talks weren't thought of as being more important than the sutras, Chinese koan collections, and other Buddhist writings. The most enthusiastic responses came from outside of the community of his students. Today there are other collections of his lectures, a couple of books about him and his teaching, more books and articles with something on him or from him, and much more on the Internet, including all his extant lectures. There are more than seventy groups in his lineage scattered around America and Europe. But Shunryu Suzuki's renown as a seminal spiritual teacher is almost entirely due to this one unique volume.

In 2004 Weatherhill, which originally published *Zen Mind, Beginner's Mind,* became an imprint of Shambhala. Now in 2010 with this special edition, Shambhala commemorates the fortieth anniversary of the publishing of these celebrated "Informal Talks on Zen Meditation and Practice."

More significant than *Zen Mind, Beginner's Mind*'s consistently impressive sales is its universal appeal. It easily moved past the perimeter of Buddhism into libraries, university classes, and reading groups. It now shows up on almost any list of modern spiritual classics in the West. Laurance Rockefeller said he kept it by his bed. Film director Sam Peckinpah opened it one evening and didn't put it down all night. Basketball coach Phil Jackson refers to it repeatedly in his book, *Sacred Hoops.* Its influence did not diminish with time. In 2000, Tosca, the Viennese "masters of deluxe soundscapes," released *Suzuki,* an album dedicated to Shunryu Suzuki. I've seen quotes from it on greeting cards, on the side of a soy milk container.

In *How the Swans Came to the Lake,* the late Rick Fields's sterling history of Western Buddhism, he wrote,

Zen Mind, Beginner's Mind had a fresh, early morning quality to it. Suzuki Roshi spoke with a spare voice, unpretentious and humorous. It was, in fact, an American Buddhist voice, unlike any heard before, and yet utterly familiar. When Suzuki Roshi spoke, it was as if American Buddhists could hear themselves perhaps for the first time.

The Buddhist scholar and Dogen translator Kazuaki Tanahashi commented, "Suzuki Roshi digested Dogen's teaching fully and presented it in his own words, so if we study Dogen and read *Zen Mind, Beginner's Mind* carefully we find an invisible but strong connection."

Many readers have a genuine and lasting affection for this book. For a couple of years, a poet named Genine Lentine with support from the San Francisco Zen Center has been working on the Page Project, in which she's collecting scans of people's personalized pages of *Zen Mind, Beginner's Mind,* with notes written in the margins, words underlined, doodles, corners folded. "Held close, passed along," she writes, "left behind, read aloud, consulted in the middle of the night, carried on the subway or bus, *Zen Mind, Beginner's Mind* seems to engage the reader in a direct and warm conversation."

A year ago, for the fiftieth anniversary of Suzuki's arrival in America, Genine created an exhibition in which each page of the book was represented by someone's contribution, culled from hundreds sent her, including pages translated into Czech, Dutch, Finnish, French, German, Icelandic, Japanese, Portuguese, Russian, Spanish, and Vietnamese. We're not sure how many languages it's been translated into. Genine says there's a student at the City Center who read it in his native Mongolian translated from the Russian version.

Genine has dedicated page 103 to "my friend Lee Briccetti, a poet and executive director of Poets House in New York. On the morning of September 11, 2001, she was on her balcony, thirty-one floors up, looking out over lower Manhattan and reading this book, and as she read the line, 'Because we cannot accept the truth of transiency, we suffer,' she heard the first plane roar overhead."

From a letter sent to the Page Project: "Amid this torment, I looked up. On my shrine sat a copy of *Zen Mind, Beginner's Mind,* with the back cover quietly lighting the cabin. Suzuki Roshi's kind and mildly humored gaze moved me to tears. I took the book from the shrine and opened it at random. I don't recall which chapter I read. Likely it wouldn't have mattered. Suzuki Roshi's words melted my struggle."

Indeed, Robert Boni's photo on the back cover of the original edition is a key ingredient. It resides on many a wall and refrigerator. The Tibetan Rinpoche Chögyam Trungpa, who called Suzuki his accidental American father, placed that photo on his group's altars along with that of his own teacher. Mrs. Suzuki, however, didn't approve of it, at least when she first saw it, and wondered aloud why a formal photo of her husband in ceremonial robes hadn't been used instead of one taken when he was in his work clothes and needed a shave.

The society photographer Yvonne Lewis used to come with her Zen student–comedian son Mark to hear Suzuki lecture in San Francisco. She commented, "Each person's face has two different sides. Suzuki Roshi had a face in

which each half was so totally different from the other that
I was fascinated by it. The side with the eyebrow up on the
Zen Mind, Beginner's Mind photo is the mischievous side and
the other is his contemplative side." Richard Baker says that
to him "the right side of his face is the calm, normal, con-
ventional person and the left side with the eyebrow up is
the enlightened side communicating, showing itself, wondering, skeptical, who are you."

The Estonian poet Jaan Kaplinski refers to this photo-
graph in a poem called "Shunryu Suzuki," translated into
English with Sam Hamill.

> Shunryu Suzuki
> a little Japanese living
> and teaching in California
> couldn't be my teacher
> one of my non-teachers
> a little lit match from God's matchbox
> sea wind soon blew out
> somewhere between California and Estonia
> somewhere between East and West
> between somewhere and nowhere
> nobody can find out what remained of him
> after the wind has blown and the tide
> come and gone—the white sand
> as smooth as before—but his smile
> from the back cover of *Zen Mind Beginner's Mind*
> has silently infected book after book on my
> shelves
> and perhaps shelves themselves and walls and
> wallpaper too

Huston Smith, the dean of world religion scholars, was an early fan of *Zen Mind, Beginner's Mind*. His preface to the book was included later, maybe when it went paperback. Expanding on what he'd written about D. T. and Shunryu back then, Huston said over the phone:

> In my introduction to *Zen Mind, Beginner's Mind* I allude to my experience with Suzuki Roshi. Any way to be affiliated with Suzuki Roshi is a joy as you understand. I wish I had more to add but I remember nothing but the wonderful aura, the peace and presentness of the man, his impact upon me. His contribution was immense. Of the two Suzukis, Daisetsu accomplished a major, major achievement by bringing Zen and, in a way, Mahayana Buddhism to America, not single-handedly, because there was Nyogen Senzaki in LA, and the First Zen Institute in New York City with Mary Farkas, but as far as the general public was concerned, almost that. And then Shunryu Suzuki comes in in a different mode, because far from the public figure that Daisetsu was, Shunryu was quiet, low key, low profile. And I do think that the two Suzukis had the most impact. I think of them as complementing each other in a very wonderful way.

Huston's comparison reminds me of how once on a bus in New York City when someone asked him if he was D. T. Suzuki, Shunryu replied that no, he's the big Suzuki, I'm the little one.

John Nelson, a professor in the department of religion at

the University of San Francisco who teaches classes on Zen and Buddhism, writes,

> What caught my attention was the combination of person, voice, and perspective. The person looked at me from the back cover as if challenging my assumptions about Zen and reality in general. His voice on the page had a unique way of expressing key ideas and explaining the commonplace so that it took on new significance. Zen was not restricted to meditation but permeated all dimensions of life and consciousness. To a young man like myself in Kansas who was sorely disillusioned by Vietnam, race and cultural conflicts, and Watergate, the book offered an entirely new perspective on reality and human behavior.

Steve Tipton, a Suzuki student who teaches sociology and religion at Emory University, wrote,

> For all the genius of its cultural and canonical translation, the practical wisdom of this book arises from its communal creation, bred by teacher and students listening and talking to each other in the course of sitting, walking, and working together every day. Through the dance of this dialogue, embodied in a way of life reborn over eons and expressed with poetic grace, comes a truly original and compassionate voice so close at hand it can open our eyes and touch our hearts.

The popularity of this book is not so much because people dwell on how great Suzuki was but because he conveys to readers that they are great. He has confidence that you, whoever you are, can understand Zen, Buddhism, reality, truth, yourself. I've interviewed and talked with hundreds of people about their experience and memories of Suzuki, and over and over so many have revealed that he (and often only he) completely understood and appreciated them. And this connection he had with people in person comes through almost like magic in *Zen Mind, Beginner's Mind*. Read the online reviews. There are now more than 150 on Amazon.com. I think they're the most telling, because they were written not by experts who had an assignment to compose reviews, but by readers who felt compelled to share their impression.

Buddhism had long been established within Asian-American communities when Suzuki arrived in San Francisco to serve as the priest for Japanese Americans at Sokoji, the city's Soto Zen temple. But only a handful of people in the West such as poet Gary Snyder had worked with a teacher and grown deeply involved with zazen. At the same time, Buddhism had been moving gradually from something lofty to admire from afar into something practical that one could integrate into one's life. *The Light of Asia,* a biography of the Buddha published in London in 1879, had sold over a million copies and been made into a movie in 1928. D. T. Suzuki's and Alan Watts's brilliant books on Zen and Buddhism were widely read. Dwight Goddard's *Buddhist Bible* inspired Jack Kerouac, and Kerouac and his Beat colleagues inspired many others. Indispensable sutras, early Buddhist texts, and commentary became available through scholars such as Edward Conze. *Zen Flesh, Zen Bones* by Paul

Reps and Nyogen Senzaki was a delight. Such skillful and devoted writing over decades had set the stage for what was to follow—people diving with body and mind into the stream of Buddhism.

Buddhist publishing was turning toward books on practice. Enlightenment was being presented as a real possibility, close enough to almost touch. In this vein, Philip Kapleau's landmark *Three Pillars of Zen* had come out in 1965, and in 1969 Chögyam Trungpa's *Meditation in Action* was published. Shunryu Suzuki brought the Soto emphasis that enlightenment and practice were one. Rick Fields nailed it with the first sentence in his chapter, "The Sixties": "'Where there is practice there is enlightenment.' This above all was the message Shunryu Suzuki-roshi brought to America." And what is practice? As Suzuki says in this book, "Instead of having some object of worship we just concentrate on the activity we do in each moment."

Zen Mind, Beginner's Mind begins with Suzuki saying that the goal of practice is always to keep our beginner's mind. Limitless and ready for anything, this Eastern tabula rasa is not, however, a blank starting point. It *is* the point. This is the "mind of purity open to things as they are" or "things as it is" as he sometimes said. Suzuki's first teacher, Gyokujun So-on, stressed the importance of beginner's mind. So had Dogen. I'm reminded of the well-known D. T. Suzuki story of the Zen master who poured tea into the overflowing cup of a visiting professor to illustrate that his guest's mind was so full of assumptions and opinions that there was no room to learn anything. And then there was the wealthy lay sage, Vimalakirti, who had his home emptied of all furnishings in order to truly receive Shakyamuni Buddha's visit. Beginner's mind is the key to awakening to big mind, a favorite term of Suzuki's—big mind, the absolute, our true nature; not small mind, the product of our "silly idea of self." One of Shunryu Suzuki's closest disciples, Silas Hoadley, remembers Suzuki saying in the early sixties, "I've come to destroy your mind." Silas realized that the mind targeted for annihilation was the ego, the small mind, a delusion to begin with, but he said it was still a chilling statement. Suzuki recalled how he and his fellow disciples were losing their beginner's mind in their teens—through innocently seeing Zen as good, special, a means to gain something. He warned about the perils of being attached to any idea, including that of beginner's mind.

We can thank Marian Derby, now Marian Wisberg, for putting together the first draft of this book, as Richard Baker notes in his introduction. Marian, known to many by her pen name, Marian Mountain, did more than that. She helped break the veritable taboo against recording Suzuki's lectures, which were thought of as only for the moment and the people at hand. Zen, he said, was passed on mind to mind. No doubt that's right, but as he also used to say, it's not always so. After six years in America, Suzuki's English had greatly improved. With his openness, his beginner's mind, he'd come to know his host country and his students more deeply. The time was ripe for him to begin to leave a record of what he sought to share.

We also have Marian's father to thank for asking a question while driving Suzuki from Los Altos to San Francisco. He asked what his personal ambition in life was, and Suzuki, surely because he was not talking to one of his students, said, "I'd like to write a book." When her father passed this on to Marian, she took it seriously. She talked to Suzuki about taping his lectures and putting together a book. He agreed. At about the same time his students in San Francisco likewise began to tape. Of what he said before that time we now have some thirty lectures, many just fragments, based on notes. But from July 1965 to his final season late in 1971, we have about 330 complete lecture transcripts, with the audio as well, for all but sixty. We're still finding tapes and transcripts not included in the known archive of his talks. Sadly, all but two of the tapes for the *Zen Mind, Beginner's Mind* lectures are lost.

Although this book contains the earliest of Suzuki's captured talks, they hold up well in comparison to those that followed. Joseph Galewsky, a Zen practitioner and professor of Earth and Planetary Sciences at the University of New Mexico, has studied and worked with the Suzuki lecture archive. He remarked that these mid-sixties talks from Los Altos, which Suzuki knew were being recorded for a book, are to him the most clear and concise of them all, "with that warm, wise way of talking about the Dharma that has become the hallmark of Suzuki Roshi's teaching."

Rinzai Zen priest Eido Shimano, who since 1965 has led the New York Zen Studies Society, proudly showed me his autographed first edition of *Zen Mind, Beginner's Mind* and with a nostalgic smile said, "I consider Suzuki Roshi not only as one of the great patriarchs of Zen in America, but also I consider myself as one of his hidden students."

Another Zen teacher who emphasized rigorous practice with koans, the late Taizan Maezumi, founder of the Zen Center of Los Angeles, said of Suzuki and his legacy, "Nobody can tell you about the past. What's important is not what happened or didn't happen back then. What's important is what we have here now. Even before this century, all kinds of priests in the Zen tradition came to America. We don't really know why, but until he came, no one started anything that lasted. After him, so much happened. That's what I most appreciate."

In 2000 Weatherhill brought out a new edition and, as with the first one, made little of it. Richard Baker, who became Suzuki's sole dharma heir in America, as well as literary executor of this book, corrected a few misunderstandings from his introduction. There were a couple of mistakes in the chapters, too, one being that Suzuki had, with customary absentmindedness, attributed the Sun-faced Buddha, Moon-faced Buddha story to Ummon (Yunmen) rather than Baso (Mazu)—and no one caught it in time or did anything about it for thirty years. I understand that the Japanese translator took Suzuki to task for that in his introduction. It hasn't done well in Japanese. He's been regarded by the Soto Zen establishment in Japan as overrated in the West, possibly because he acted on his own, not within or through their system of which he was quite critical.

Fred Harriman, a brilliant translator I've worked with, whom I regard as an expert on things Japanese, says that in time they will inevitably come to recognize Shunryu Suzuki in his homeland, because what he accomplished is very important to them: he brought something completely Japanese to the West and successfully planted it here.

As Maezumi pointed out, we don't really know what happened in the past, but as I see it, a team of people heeded their highest angels to create this book. Marian came up with a manuscript entitled "Beginner's Mind" in which she had minimally edited most of the lectures she'd recorded. Suzuki suggested she pass the manuscript on to Richard so he could edit it. She gave it to him in March of 1967 just as Tassajara was preparing for the first practice period. When he finally read it the following fall, he agreed it was good material for a book. He worked with it awhile, but was busy with the growing Zen Center and its fundraising efforts and turned for help to Trudy Dixon, a Wellesley graduate who'd also done graduate studies in philosophy at UC Berkeley. She agreed, even though she was married with two young children and was dealing with breast cancer.

The result was a close collaboration. Trudy and Richard would each meet with Suzuki to clarify what he meant in particular passages and they would also meet together to discuss how best to express his meaning. Trudy devoted the last working energy of her life to this book—honing the language, organizing the talks into three sections and deciding on the quotation headings. As she was dying she continued to sit zazen, until it became reclining zazen, and finally lying down zazen. She is remembered for her intelligence, spirit, and courage.

In October of 1968, at Suzuki's request, Baker sailed for Japan to further study Zen and the culture it was wrapped in. He went with his wife and daughter, and the nearly completed manuscript. In Tokyo he would find the publisher.

Before me is the unedited transcript of a lecture that Suzuki gave in November of 1965. A sentence in it reads, "In beginner's mind we have many possibilities, but in expert mind there is not much possibility." In the book, through various stages of editing, that became the often quoted, "In the beginner's mind there are many possibilities, but in the expert's there are few." The message is unchanged but it reads better.

"I read Zen Mind, Beginner's Mind," Suzuki said once, "to see what the understanding of my disciples is."

On that day when the books arrived, Suzuki looked one over, made light of it, hung out awhile, and went with his wife back upstairs to their rooms.

David Chadwick is the author of Crooked Cucumber: The Life and Zen Teaching of Shunryu Suzuki *(Broadway, 1999), and* Zen Is Right Here: Teaching Stories and Anecdotes of Shunryu Suzuki, Author of Zen Mind, Beginner's Mind *(Shambhala Publications, 2007).*

Sources for the quotes in this article, notes, and extensive elaboration can be found at http://zmbm.net.

SHUNRYU SUZUKI (1904–1971) was one of the most influential spiritual teachers of the twentieth century and is truly a founding father of Zen in America. A Japanese priest of the Soto lineage, he taught in the United States from 1959 until his death. He was the founder of the San Francisco Zen Center and the Tassajara Zen Mountain Center. He is also the author of *Branching Streams Flow in the Darkness: Zen Talks on the Sandokai,* and he is the subject of the biography *Crooked Cucumber*.